THE TELEVISION NEWS INTERVIEW

The SAGE CommText Series

Series Editor:
EVERETTE E. DENNIS
Gannett Center for Media Studies, Columbia University

Founding Editor: F. GERALD KLINE, *late of the School of Journalism and Mass Communication, University of Minnesota*
Founding Associate Editor: SUSAN H. EVANS, *Annenberg School of Communications, University of Southern California*

The **SAGE CommText** series brings the substance of mass communication scholarship to student audiences by blending syntheses of current research with applied ideas in concise, moderately priced volumes. Designed for use both as supplementary readings and as "modules" with which the teacher can "create" a new text, the **SAGE CommTexts** give students a conceptual map of the field of communication and media research. Some books examine topical areas and issues; others discuss the implications of particular media; still others treat methods and tools used by communication scholars. Written by leading researchers with the student in mind, the **SAGE CommTexts** provide teachers in communication and journalism with solid supplementary materials.

Available in this series:

additional titles in preparation

Akiba A. Cohen

THE
TELEVISION
NEWS INTERVIEW

Volume 18. The Sage CommText Series

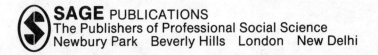

SAGE PUBLICATIONS
The Publishers of Professional Social Science
Newbury Park   Beverly Hills   London   New Delhi

To my parents, Ethel and Abraham Cohen

For information address:

SAGE Publications, Inc.
2111 West Hillcrest Drive
Newbury Park, California 91320

SAGE Publications Inc.
275 South Beverly Drive
Beverly Hills
California 90212

SAGE Publications Ltd.
28 Banner Street
London EC1Y 8QE
England

SAGE PUBLICATIONS India Pvt. Ltd.
M-32 Market
Greater Kailash I
New Delhi 110 048 India

Printed in the United States of America

Library of Congress Catologing-in-Publication Data

Cohen, Akiba A.
  The television news interview.

  (The Sage commtext series ; v. 18)
  Bibliography: p.
  Includes index.
  1. Interviewing in television. 2. Television
broadcasting of news. I. Title. II. Series.
PN1992.8.I68C64   1987   070.1'9   87-13025
ISBN 0-8039-2594-8
ISBN 0-8039-2595-6 (pbk.)

CONTENTS

ACKNOWLEDGMENTS

This book is the outcome of a growing curiosity about television news interviewing. It began while working on another study of television news in several countries. It seemed to me that while many characteristics of news in various countries were rather similar, the interviews appeared to be quite different. I began asking myself why, and this book is the result.

I would like to thank Hanna Adoni, Charles Bantz, Deanna Robinson, Gabriele Bock, Friedrich Knilli, Jay Blumler, Michael Gurevitch, Alison Ewbank, and Karen Honikman, my colleagues in the other news study for enabling me to use the raw data that we collected together. I owe much thanks to the many news reporters and producers whom I interviewed for this book in the United States, Britain, West Germany, and Israel; their names and affiliations are listed in the text. They provided me with their time, hospitality, and most important, with their important personal insights into what they do so often. Credit is also due to my students in Jerusalem who added important comments and suggestions in the course of two seminars on the subject of the book. I also wish to acknowledge my colleague, Moshe Zimmermann, who assisted me in interpreting the German newscasts. I owe much gratitude to Mark R. Levy, of the the University of Maryland, who reviewed the manuscript and contributed numerous insights and compelled me to rethink some of the points I made. And finally, I wish to thank Everette E. Dennis, my editor, who showed much patience and understanding, despite the long distances and the time it took the mail to cross the Atlantic.

Most of all, I wish to thank my wife, Esther, and children Orlee and Amitai, three people who displayed much tolerance when I was busy watching the news. As Amitai, who was only six, kept saying, "Aren't you bored watching that stuff again and again?"

Akiba A. Cohen
Jerusalem, Israel

PREFACE

This book is about television news interviewing, a brief but significant part of most newscasts. It usually involves verbal and visual information presented to the viewer following research, field work, interaction between individuals, as well as filming, recording, editing, and many decisions along the way. Despite the fact that much of television news in the Western world is very similar in structure and content, the news interview is used differently in the various countries. This, then, is what makes it rather special: It reflects the society, the individual in it, and the reciprocal relationship between the news source, the newsperson and the cultural context in which news is gathered and produced. In other words, if we could imagine a set of concentric circles, the inner most of which is the news interview itself, surrounded in turn by television news, television, the media, and finally by culture or society, we may be correct in suggesting that the television news interview encapsulates some elements of its surrounding circles, which include political norms, social relationships, aesthetic values, and rules of etiquette, just to mention a few.

My approach to the topic of the television news interview is from three perspectives. First, the theoretical perspective, which includes a taxonomy of journalistic interviewing, a discussion on the nature of television interviewing, as well as a review of the meager literature on the topic. The second perspective is empirical, based on a comparative content-analytic study of how interviewing is done in the newscasts of four countries—The United States, Britain, West Germany, and Israel. And third, a confirmatory perspective, based on interviews I conducted with experienced television news reporters and producers in the four countries, who have conducted many interviews and who were able to provide important insights into the rationale and the process of interviewing in the news. In bringing them together I attempt to discuss some of the inherent problems with the television news interview and some avenues that it might take.

The book emphasizes the comparative approach. I strongly believe that this approach is highly effective in providing meaning to any phenomenon. The crucial point is to determine what criteria to use in doing the comparison. Indeed, this volume contains several levels of comparison. It begins with a discussion of what makes the journalistic interview unique among other forms of interviewing. It then examines the television interview within the context of journalistic interviewing. The third stage is an explication of the different kinds of television interviews, and the narrowing in on the television news interview. Then, following a review of the literature, two empirical comparisons are made: among the three U.S. commercial networks and among the American, British, German, and Israeli major evening newscasts. The final section of the book is an attempt to explain the similarities and differences and to suggest where the television news interview ought to be going.

This book is not a traditional textbook that tries to teach interviewing in a "how to do it" sense. It is instead a study of interviewing for students, researchers, and the press. Contrary to Gaye Tuchman's famous article (1974) entitled "Making News by Doing Work: Routinizing the Unexpected," in which she claims that the news media adapt fixed and standard ways of dealing with events in the course of creating the news, I would like to suggest that news interviewing is not a mindless and "routine" process in news making. This may be the case for several reasons, the most important of which is that it is a situation where the news organization comes in contact with people, different kinds of people, thereby making the newsperson take into account the idiosyncratic characteristics of the interviewee and the situation. It is a product of planned interaction conditioned by personalities and context.

This book is not intended to teach how to conduct a news interview, at least not in a direct way. It is my belief, however, that by discovering how interviewing is done in television news, and especially how it is done in more than one place, one can gain important understanding of what it is all about, its potential uses, and possible pitfalls. Using this information, together with a standard textbook as well as practical training, it is hoped that the student of broadcast news as well as the professional journalist will gain additional insight and understanding of this fascinating phenomenon.

1

DIMENSIONS OF
THE JOURNALISTIC INTERVIEW

What are the special characteristics of the journalistic interview—print and electronic—and how does it differ from other kinds of interviews? What are the pressures and constraints of television interviews?

Webster's Collegiate Dictionary provides two definitions of the term *interview*. In the first, an interview is "a mutual sight or view; a meeting face to face; usually, a formal consultation." The second definition has a more direct bearing on our present topic: "A meeting between a representative of the press with a person from whom he seeks information for publication; also, the press article giving this information." Although interviews are used in many fields, for example, in personnel work, medicine, clinical psychology, social work, law, and social research (including public opinion polling and marketing research), only the journalistic interview receives special mention in the dictionary. Certainly it is the most visible form of the interview, although most people probably have greater experience on the receiving end in the personnel or medical interview.

Much of the information collected by journalists in the course of their work is based on interviewing. However, not all the information gathered by reporters in the course of interviews is actually used in a direct and overt manner in the stories they produce. This may be due in part simply to space or time limitations, or sometimes an interview is used for background information only and it is not expected to be used directly by the reporter. In any event, it is safe to say that the interview is a central tool in the journalistic profession.

The importance and centrality of the interview in the work of the print and broadcast journalist is reflected in several books that have been written on the topic. Most of these books, as well as several chapters, mainly in, but not limited to, journalism and broadcasting handbooks and reporting texts, stress the "how to" aspects of journalistic interviewing rather than the conceptual aspects of the interview, its context, and implications. Much of the "how to" material is based on personal experiences and general impressions. As we know, in journalism as in other fields, much can be learned from the systematic study of professional practice. Such study brings together evidence from which broad generalized principles can be developed. The value of theory and research to professional practice is well known in virtually every field from business and the sciences to law. Still, it is not unusual for some professional journalists to reject research and scholarly work as impractical and not pertinent to their work. This book attempts to demonstrate the very real value of study and analysis to advancing the state of journalistic interviewing, believing that through understanding can come more enlightened and knowledgeable practice.

There is, as has been suggested, a growing body of *research* literature in journalism and broadcasting, but very little significant attention has been devoted to the study of the interview itself. On the other hand, many general texts as well as numerous research articles on interviewing in fields other than journalism have been written. Many of these books and articles present theoretical and empirical aspects of the interview as well as the training of interviewers. Unhappily, this voluminous general literature about interviewing pays little if any attention to the journalistic interview. One notable exception is a book by Kahn and Cannell (1957), in which the authors devote less than one-half of one page to the journalistic interview. The fact that the general literature on interviewing does not deal with the journalistic interview seems to be surprising for two reasons. First, it seems likely that most people in modern Western societies are more familiar, at least in a passive manner, with journalistic interviewing than with any other form of interviewing. Most of us are probably somewhat familiar with the clinical interview, such as that conducted by physicians or psychologists. In these situations the professional person or *interviewer* is interested in getting information necessary for the diagnosis and treatment of the person seeking help, the *interviewee*. Another familiar situation is the job interview. We might also have been asked to respond to questions in a poll or survey conducted by a university or marketing opinion firm. However, very few of us have actually been interviewed personally by the mass media, particularly by television. And yet, we have a vivid acquaintance with the journalistic interview by virtue of our roles as readers, listeners, and viewers. Even so, true understanding of the journalistic interview, especially television interviews, requires thoughtful analyses and even study, as this book indicates.

Why should a student of journalism, broadcasting, or mass communication be interested in the interview? There are several reasons: First, television news is one of the more complex forms of media programming; second, television news is often crucial in establishing and maintaining the reputation and credibility of television stations, if not entire networks; and third, the interview is an important tool in information gathering for news programs. Thus it seems highly desirable for sensitive students to be aware of the "philosophy" of the interview, the various ways in which it is to be done, its pitfalls and possibilities. This will help enable the student to better decipher a news interview on television and this may contribute to *media literacy,* or more specifically, *news literacy.*

On the "active" side of things, there is also practical advice here. Because interviewing is learned by doing and practical training and practice is imperative to becoming a good interviewer, no book can substitute for that. However, the information in this volume will be useful in translating some theory into practice. It has been suggested that even top-ranking journalists who are well known for their journalistic achievements are often at a loss to describe and "verbalize" the ways according to which they do their work and make their decisions. Thus, for example, reporters always speak of the "news value" of certain events as a determining factor in including reports about those events in the newscast, and yet when asked to explain or to define what is in the stories that gives them their so-called news value, they can at best merely provide examples on a case-by-case basis, thereby suggesting that some inductive process is at work. However, it is our objective to specify more clearly what those processes are and how they develop.

This book, then, will not teach all there is to know about conducting news interviews, but it should be a useful map of what is known about this important form of communication. In my experience as a teacher of communication, some of my finest students were those with some professional experience as journalists who then used theoretical approaches to provide a more meaningful context for their work. Thus bringing together theory and practice in the field of journalism in general, and in television news in particular, seems to have real value and utility. After all is said and done, what makes for a distinctive and successful interviewer is probably well beyond what academics and professionals can teach and write about, or what professional training and extensive experience can provide. There must also be operating elements of personal style, psychological disposition, maturity, and overall intelligence, which are at the core of the success of such people as Barbara Walters, Ted Koppel, and Mike Wallace, all of whom in their own special ways have captured the imagination, while sometimes delighting or enraging, millions of viewers.

This chapter discusses the journalistic interview in general terms and attempts to show how it differs from other kinds of interviews. Ultimately, the aim of this book is to point out the special attributes and characteristics of the television news interview, and to show how this unique form of communication is used by the television medium. Throughout the book the main focus is interviewing as it is actually done on the evening news programs of the three commercial networks of American television, which are models for local stations and for television journalists everywhere. There is also a chapter on television news interviews in several other countries. I have done this because a comparative yardstick gives us a much deeper understanding of the nature, purpose, and implications of interviewing in television news. I believe—and there is much evidence to support this idea—that the cross-cultural (or cross-national) perspective has great utility and power even if the main purpose is to understand one's own system.

THE DIMENSIONS OF THE
JOURNALISTIC INTERVIEW

All interviews are social encounters. All interviews involve at least two persons performing specific roles, that of *interviewer* and that of *interviewee*. During the course of an interview questions are posed by the interviewer to the interviewee in order to obtain information. The nature of the information exhibited can be verbal or nonverbal. The information can be factual or attitudinal. Finally, there can be various reasons why interviewees submit themselves to an interrogation by another individual. All of these points seem to indicate that there is good reason to consider the interview as a special form of interaction, with social and psychological implications.

As I have suggested, in order to argue that something is unique, it must be compared with something else. One way to do this is to compare the *journalistic* interview to other kinds of interviews, such as the clinical interview, the job interview, the legal interview, and the research interview, which also happen to be the kinds of interviews most discussed in the general literature on interviewing.

What follows, then, are several dimensions against which the journalistic interview may be compared with the nonjournalistic interview. These dimensions do not exhaust all the possibilities, nor are they completely mutually exclusive of one another. They do demonstrate ways the journalistic interview differs significantly from other forms of interviewing. The use of these dimensions enables us to place the journalistic interview in context. By doing so we shall hopefully be able to determine to what extent, and under what circumstances, the journalistic interview is similar to or different from the nonjournalistic interview.

Moreover, in presenting each of these dimensions, I do not suggest that the journalistic interview is totally different or unique from the other kinds of interviewing. It is not a case of one versus all the others. Instead, there are gradations of emphasis in each of these dimensions, and thus the dimensions can serve as useful tools to clarify and highlight the characteristics of the journalistic interview. In other words, these dimensions and the position that the journalistic interview occupies on each continuum derived from them should be considered, at least for the present time, as tentative and hypothetical, yet worthy of empirical examination.

One additional caveat: All of the dimensions I present below are related to the interview process, the interviewer(s), and the inter-viewee(s). In fact, this book presents the television news interview from the perspectives of the content of the interview, its origins, formats, and constraints. The purpose of these dimensions, then, is *not* to develop a typology of the possible *effects* of the interview as presented in newspapers, radio, or television on readers, listeners, or viewers, even though the effects of the interview is an important topic with which we are also concerned. Indeed, I would like to suggest that the various ways in which the interviews are conducted and presented on the screen might have different consequences for different audiences. We are interested, for example, in some of the effects of the television news interview, such as the possible effects on the audience of hearing or not hearing the question that the interviewee is asked; thus, does hearing or not hearing the questions affect the comprehension of what was said in the course of the interview? However, since this book is empirically based, and very little, if any, research evidence is available on which to base such conclusions, we must suffice at this point in time with healthy speculation about the possible impact, effects, and consequences of interviews and interviewing.

The Interview as a Goal
or as a Means to a Goal

All interviews involve interpersonal communication aimed at eliciting information. In this sense the task of the journalist, the psychologist, the employer, the social researcher, and various other professionals is quite similar. And yet, if we examine the underlying reason that the interview is conducted, it will become evident that in the case of the psychologist, the employer, or the researcher, the interview is actually a means toward some more distant goal, namely deciding on a technique for therapy, whether or not to hire the prospective worker, or to generate research data, respectively. These interviews are a starting point for a longer and more involved transaction.

In some cases, however, the journalistic interview is conducted as a goal in itself. This is often from the point of view of the journalist, and sometimes from the point of view of the person being interviewed. It is not uncommon for a journalist to be credited, mainly by colleagues and sometimes even by the public, simply for having obtained the interview without much consideration of what was said in it and its possible implications. In fact, getting an interview with a usually unavailable person can be the topic of a news story even if the interview yielded little new information. This does not mean that no journalistic interviews are conducted with some more distant goal in mind. Indeed, most journalistic interviews are done to expose an issue or get background material. Some interviews are done for background purposes only and are not published or broadcast at all. Nonetheless, some interviews are conducted by journalists for the purpose of "getting the interview" and thereby receiving professional credit and rewards, mainly from colleagues.

Taking the Initiative
for the Interview

In most professional interviews such as in medicine, law, employment, and the like, it is the "client" who takes the initiative to arrange for an interview. Thus, for example, it is the patient who goes to the doctor's office with some medical complaint; it is the person looking for a job who approaches the prospective employer (whether or not a job was advertised); and it is the person accused of a crime who goes to the lawyer seeking legal advice. On the other hand, in the case of interviewing for social research, such as polling or market surveys, it is the researcher who takes the initiative to arrange for the interviews that are needed in the research project.

In the case of the journalistic interview, however, both directions of initiative-taking are possible. The best example, of course, is the case of the interview with a politician. Part of the notion of reciprocity between politicians and the press is the question of who approaches whom with a story: Is it the reporter who wants to question the politician about some issue or is it the politician who wishes to "offer" the reporter some information (whether this is done directly or indirectly via some "connection" or public relations person)? It is obviously impossible to tell how often each approach occurs, since both the reporters and politicians are generally quite reluctant to talk about this aspect of their mutual relationships, but surely both forms of interaction occur regularly.

The Professional-Expert Roles of the Participants

All interviews involve at least two persons in two distinct roles, that of interviewer and interviewee. In nonjournalistic professional interviews, the client-interviewee may happen to be a professional person or an expert (for instance, the patient may be another professional person, perhaps even another doctor), or the client may be a nonprofessional person. The same is true for other interviews such as with psychologists, lawyers, social workers, employers, and social researchers. In most instances, however, in nonjournalistic professional interviews, the interviewee is a nonprofessional simply because most people in society are nonprofessionals or nonexperts.

The situation with the journalistic interview is usually the reverse. In this case, most interviews are conducted with professional people who are considered expert sources of news and information (such as politicians, lawyers, doctors, university professors, artists, writers, and researchers) and only with a relatively small number of nonexpert people such as "simple" workers, homemakers, and the "man in the street." Moreover, even in the latter cases, one may consider a housewife in the supermarket or the "man in the street" being interviewed as fulfilling a temporary "professional" role as he or she possesses some degree of expertise, which is the reason he or she is approached by the journalist in the first place.

Thus assuming for the moment, that the journalist-interviewer can be considered as an expert (a point that may be disputed by people who claim that at best they tend to be generalists who "can cover anything"), we are then often faced with a situation of one expert versus another. This point can have important implications about how the interview is conducted.

The Social Status and Credibility of the Participants

The social status and credibility of most people who conduct formal interviews is far from the bottom of the social status ladder. Thus doctors, lawyers, social workers, and researchers generally rank quite high in the social hierarchy, although there might be some difference among them. Their clients or subjects, on the other hand, can be people of all walks of life.

Journalistic interviewers, as individuals, also seem to rank particularly high (although the journalism profession might not always be perceived to be top-ranked). Sometimes their credibility is due to their own personal style and achievement and sometimes it is linked to the status and credibility of the newspaper or broadcast station (or network) they represent. To a large extent their credibility and social position must be reestablished and maintained over time, and this can be done only as long as they continue to perform as expected by their readers and audiences. Interviewers on national television or even on local stations are among the elite of society, often feared and revered by millions, a fact that puts them in a special position with their interviewees. This is not only true for such national celebrities as Tom Brokaw, Peter Jennings, or Dan Rather, but for some local journalists who have considerable prestige and clout. This can be seen, for example, on enormous billboards in many cities that refer to the personal abilities of the reporters and news teams of the various local network affiliates. Indeed, this gives them celebrity status.

Contrary to the case of other professional interviews, most journalistic interviewees are from among the top-ranking echelons of society: politicians, businessmen, artists, and so on, although sometimes, as noted, the interviewee is of the "working class" or the "person in the street." Indeed, most interviewees consider themselves to be of some social importance, and they most likely believe that what they have to say is important and noteworthy. Moreover, when it does happens that a person of relatively low social status is selected to be interviewed by the media, this mere fact tends to enhance that person's self-esteem as well as his or her status in the eyes of others.

Thus the relatively high social status of both parties to the interview, combined with the "professional" roles they both fulfill in the context of the interview, may create some unique relationships that are nonexistent in nonjournalistic interviews. For example, the power relationships between two persons of "real" or even "presumed" high social rank might be potentially difficult to manage, since there might not be clear understanding as to who is "up" and who is "down" in the encounter. Even if the interviewer has taken the initiative, as is the case in most journalistic interviews, the interviewee might attempt to command the situation, and to use his or her status as a convenient pretext for such behavior.

What can sometimes make this dimension of the journalistic interview even more dynamic is the fact that some interviews are conducted with more than one interviewer or more than one interviewee. In such situations, it is not uncommon to witness competition between the interviewers in their attempts to get their questions posed to the interviewee(s). Also, there can be competition between the interviewees in their attempts to provide the answers to the questions and thereby impress the audience.

Representativeness in Selecting Interviewees

In most professional nonjournalistic interviews there are no rules employed by the interviewer for selecting a particular interviewee since it is the interviewee who seeks to be interviewed because of some need he or she has. This is also the case in journalistic interviews when, for example, a politician approaches a reporter and asks to be interviewed. However, when the journalist chooses the interviewee, this can be done according to one of two general rules. The interviewee may be the subject of the story or report, in which case the choice of that particular person is obvious and self-evident. Thus, for example, a particular politician can be approached for an interview because the reporter is doing a story on some issue directly involving that particular individual, or because he or she may have a vested interest in the event being reported.

The second rule for choosing interviewees is based on the principle of "representativeness." Numerous news reports concern events that are witnessed by more than one person or that concern more than one person (for instance, victims of some accident or disaster). In such cases the newsperson must decide which of the possible witnesses or involved people should be approached. Several factors may determine this kind of decision, including the extent of knowledge the person has about the issue and the person's ability to be articulate and tell what happened in a concise and intelligible manner. Not every prospective interviewee would necessarily fit the prescription sought by the reporter. The question then becomes to what extent the person interviewed is "representative" of all those who could have been interviewed. Each person would tell a somewhat different story if he or she was a witness to a crime or a fire, for example, as often happens in a court of law. Another example is the selection of a particular member of Congress to be interviewed on a specific topic. On some issues it is clear that a certain senator or representative would be approached if the issue concerns that particular person. But if several or many could have been selected, the question is whether or not the person actually chosen represents the others.

In survey research, highly sophisticated sampling techniques are used to select respondents to be interviewed in order to obtain a representative sample of the population that the researcher wishes to study. In journalistic interviewing there is often a situation in which the reporter wishes to present the position of a "representative" of a particular social group such as consumers, voters, strikers, or simply the "man in the street." With this goal in mind the interviewer "selects" someone to be the "representative" person. No scientific sampling rules are adhered to and the number of interviewees is always very small, sometimes only one person. This can mean that the person selected to be interviewed is highly stereotypical, which could result in clear bias.

Advocating the Interviewer's Position

The objective of most interviews is to solicit factual information or opinions from the interviewee. The interviewer generally assumes the role of questioner and tends not to express his or her opinion, at least not in the ongoing process of the interview (except for professional advice, which may be given by the physician, lawyer, and the like, which is, after all, the reason for the interview itself). In survey research, such as polling, the interviewer is specifically trained and instructed to avoid making his or her position known to the respondent to avoid biasing his or her responses.

In the case of the journalistic interview, however, the reporter often has well defined opinions that he or she expresses in the course of the interview. This can be done overtly in a direct manner or by the use of some subtle verbal hint or suggestion or even by the use of a nonverbal gesture such as a smile, the raising of an eyebrow, or the like. Sometimes the interviewer advocates his or her personal position intentionally and sometimes the expression of the interviewer's position may be unconscious and unintentional. In either case it can be evident, at least by the interviewee or the audience.

As a result of these particular circumstances it may happen in the course of the journalistic interview that a "role reversal" will take place in which the interviewee begins to ask the reporter questions, not merely to solicit advice or information as in a medical, legal, or employment situation, but to "retaliate" and oppose the position explicitly or implicitly expressed by the interviewer.

The Confidentiality and Publicity
of the Interview

Most topics in interviews with doctors, psychologists, lawyers, and so on, are personal in nature and are, therefore, considered private and confidential. Also, a respondent in a marketing survey or public opinion poll is usually guaranteed anonymity. A patient, a welfare recipient, a survey respondent, a job applicant, and other persons being interviewed have some degree of ego involvement or self-esteem "hanging on the line" during the course of the interview. The same is true about the professional conducting the interview. Any failure on the part of either of the participants is detrimental either in the short run or in the long run. Thus most of these interviews are held in private, far from the limelight, with no possibility for public scrutiny of what was said and how it was said.

However, when a person consents to be interviewed for the media, the interviewee cannot generally expect to benefit from confidentiality. Thus not only is *what* the person says in the interview made public, but the person *himself* or *herself* is exposed publicly. Indeed, there are occasions when the voice of the interviewee is modified or the camera shoots the interviewee in such a way as to disguise his or her identity. This is done when there is imminent threat to the interviewee or when there is good reason to protect his or her identity. It is also common journalistic practice to protect the identity of the journalist's source when the information obtained is intended for background only or for "off the record" statements, having reached consensus on this prior to the interview.

And yet, with few exceptions the essence of the journalistic interview potentially involves total or nearly total exposure, both in terms of what was said and of how the interview was conducted. This is despite the fact that the journalist does not or cannot always go into detail as to the circumstances in which the interview was conducted. Nonetheless, this information is often presented by the print journalist in writing; also often it can be heard or seen by the audience of the electronic media. What is most important, however, is that what was said cannot be fully retracted, and that the impression that the interviewer and interviewee make is difficult, if not impossible, to rectify. The participants are aware of this constraint of the interviewing situation and must take it into account when they agree to engage in the interviewing process.

The Accuracy of Interview Protocols

During or following most interviews some document called a "protocol" is prepared which is intended as a record of what transpired during the interview. Thus, for example, a protocol of a medical or psychological interview includes the basic information that the patient provided concerning symptoms, feelings, and so on. The format of the protocol may be standard for all patients or it may be only partially standardized. At the conclusion of a job interview, for instance, the interviewer usually prepares a summary of the interview that describes his or her impression of the applicant and the basic things that were said in the course of the interview. These protocols are usually filed for future access, in some regular fashion, as needed. As for social research, the instrument being used, namely, the interview schedule (or question-naire) is used either in its raw form or it is analyzed according to some uniform set of rules, and then it is combined with the information gathered from the other interviewees-respondents.

In the case of the journalistic interview, there is no standardized way of preparing a protocol. No special forms are used, thus one protocol does not necessarily resemble another. The protocol (or interview notes) may be filed away in some fashion, but this is not always the case. What is critical, however, in the protocol of the journalistic interview is the widely growing practice of electronically recording what the interviewee said, word for word, so as to be able to quote exactly what he or she said. This is particularly important, since the exact words used in interviews, especially by prominent people, and concerning socially important issues, can make a significant difference if they are misquoted or taken out of context. In a sense, then, the protocol or recording of the interview session becomes the "interview" itself, the product or text that is the *raison d'etre* for the whole interaction. This does not mean that in other forms of interviewing the accuracy of the protocols is unimportant; however, given the nature of journalism with its special social impact, there is a strong emphasis on a highly authentic protocol.

The Social Impact of the Interview

In most cases of professional interviewing there is relatively little social impact of the interview beyond the scope of the person being interviewed and his or her family or immediate social and personal environment. Thus, for example, a patient may be the immediate beneficiary of the clinical interview, and his or her immediate social environment might be affected. The same can be said of the job interview, the legal interview, and so on.

By its very nature, however, the public journalistic interview that is often read, heard or seen by millions of people, exactly at or shortly after the time it is made, usually has a much wider scope of influence and possible repercussions. This is the case when a high-ranking politician is interviewed about some important topic of the day, interviews with labor leaders, victims of crime or disaster, as well as interviewees fulfilling many other significant social roles. Therefore, the journalistic interview must be considered a medium of important social influence and potential social impact.

The Potential Longevity of the Interviewer-Interviewee Relationship

The context in which the typical nonjournalistic interview is conducted is well defined. That is, the patient comes to the doctor or the psychologist to be cured, the job applicant comes for an employment interview in order to get a job, the accused person comes to a lawyer to get legal help, the pollster knocks on the door (or phones) to get specific information, and so forth. Thus when the purpose for which the professional-interviewer and the client-interviewee engage in the encounter has been achieved, or if and when it is determined that the goal cannot be obtained, the relationship is terminated. This occurs regardless of whether the relationship was long (sometimes lasting even years in the case of clinical psychology) or whether it was brief (as in the case of a public opinion survey). Once the relationship between the interview participants is over, there is generally no expectancy on the part of either one of them that they have an obligation toward the other and the chance that they will meet in another interviewing situation is relatively remote. It is possible, of course, that a patient may become ill again or a person might seek legal counsel at some other occasion, thereby reestablishing the relationship with the same professional.

However, in the case of the journalistic interview, there is a much greater likelihood that the relationship following a given interview will endure. This is particularly the case with politicians, government officials, civil servants, and various experts. Thus when a reporter interviews a politician, for example, he or she must consider the possibility that following the interview, and based on how it was conducted as well as its consequences, there may be another interview between the two at some point in the future. The nature of the reciprocity and expectations between the interviewee and the journalist are such that there is always this potential for renewed contact that influences the way each interview encounter takes place. Of course the extent to which the longevity of the reporter-source relationship will be maintained differs from one setting to another; thus, for example, it is more likely that these relationships will endure for a longer period of time at the national news level compared with the local level where "beats" are not all that common.

Time and Space Constraints

Most interviews are scheduled and conducted within a specified time frame. The patient seeking help from his doctor or the client from his lawyer usually schedules an appointment. In many cases, the scheduling is not one of an "emergency," although such crisis situations obviously do occur from time to time.

The journalistic interview operates within several forms of time constraint. First, the journalistic interview is very often related to events that occur unexpectedly so that advanced scheduling is very frequently impossible. This sense of urgency that drives many journalists puts much pressure on the journalist and the prospective interviewee. Both would like to have time to prepare for the interview, they would like to get their information sorted out, and have their ideas organized in a presentable manner. However, given the circumstances, this is not always possible. As a matter of fact, it is often the case that the journalist wishes to obtain the interview in a manner that will purposely not allow the interviewee to prepare so that he or she might be caught off guard. This is even considered by some to be one of the ingredients of a good story.

The second form of time constraint has to do with the length of the interviewing session itself. In the nonjournalistic interview, additional sessions can usually be scheduled if there is not enough time available to complete the interview in the time allotted for it. In the journalistic interview, on the other hand, it is often impossible, due to the nature of the event and the identity of the interviewee (for example, high ranking official, foreign dignitary, and so on) to schedule another session.

The final form of constraint has to do with the actual time slot in the broadcast media or the space available in the printed media. The interviewer is usually given a certain amount of time or space for the completed "product," with little or no flexibility left to his or her discretion. This places pressure both on the interviewer as well as on the interviewee, even in prerecorded interviews that are then edited for presentation to the audience, and especially in live interviews. Both parties must express their positions while taking the time constraint into account, which is often quite difficult to accomplish. Whereas the interviewer-journalist is usually trained and has experience to count on, the interviewee is often not accustomed to this type of situation. Of course some interviewees, mainly politicians, who have had debate training, learn to make their case in a succinct manner, but there are many who find this quite difficult.

The Location of the Interview

Most professional interviews are conducted in a quiet and private setting, familiar at least to one of the participants. Thus, for example, the doctor, lawyer, psychologist, or social worker are quite accustomed to their environment when they conduct the interview within the confines of their office. Indeed, the patient or client may be initially inconvenienced by the unfamiliar setting, but as time goes by, and if additional sessions are required, the interviewee manages to get better acquainted with the new environment and tends to feel more comfortable. However, there are situations, for example, when the lawyer interviews the client in jail or the social worker conducts the interview in the home of the welfare person, in which case the interviewer is the party who needs to adjust to the new setting. And yet, it is assumed that these professionals have learned in the course of their training to deal with these special settings. Finally, in the case of the research interview, the respondent is generally in a familiar environment—home, office, or place of work, and it is the interviewer who must move from location to location and become adjusted to each new setting. In short, in the nonjournalistic interview setting at least one of the parties is on his or her own turf.

In the journalistic interview, however, the setting frequently changes both for the interviewer and the interviewee. Thus the reporter will need to approach his interviewees in various locations, in an office, in a studio, indoors or out of doors, in friendly or hostile surroundings, and at times even in secret hiding places or retreats. The interviewee, for his or her part, particularly for a broadcast interview, might meet on his or her own turf, or might need to come to an unfamiliar setting such as a radio or television studio and need to relate not only to the interviewer, but to other people such as technicians and directors. The interviewee will also need to become familiar with artifacts such as the microphone, the presence of a camera, bright lights, and the like. All these factors clearly might influence the "performance" of the interviewee during the course of the interview.

THE PRESSURES OF THE
TELEVISION INTERVIEW

Having considered all journalistic interviews as one general form of interviewing, let us now focus on the television interview to determine what distinguishes it from other journalistic interviews conducted for radio and newspapers. To do so, let us refer to the 12 dimensions of the journalistic interview, which I have just explicated, and let us examine in somewhat more detail some of the points particularly relevant to the *television* interview. At this point of the discussion let us consider the entire array of television interviews as one genre. In the next chapter we shall differentiate between the various kinds of television interviews.

At the outset I wish to stress that not all 12 dimensions indicate or suggest any unique characteristics of the television interview. For instance, the question of whether or not the journalistic interview is a goal in itself or a means to a goal is not particular to the television interview. The same dilemma can be brought up with regard to radio and newspaper interviews. The issue of who takes the initiative, the journalist or the interviewee, seems to be as relevant to television as it is to the other media. The same can be said concerning the juxtaposition of the interviewer versus the interviewee and reciprocity of the professional relationships in the journalistic interview, the randomness in the selection of the interviewees, the extent to which the interviewer's position is advocated, and the longevity of the interviewer-interviewee relationship.

Of the dimensions presented in this chapter, the first that poses a more difficult situation for television interviewing compared with radio and newspaper interviewing concerns the *social status of the participants*. It can be safely argued that the social status of the leading television personalities, including reporters, both at the national and local levels, is quite high. This is part of what is meant by the notion of "TV stars" and what is referred to when dealing with the credibility of the television reporter. Although the concepts of "stardom" and "credibility" are not synonymous, they are related. They both imply prestige, although stardom has more to do with professional conduct. In any event, the prestige accorded to television personalities is the result, at least in part, of the fact that they come in close and frequent contact with persons in other high-ranking social positions such as government, politics, sports, the arts, and show business. Most people who fulfill the role of interviewee on television come from these high socially ranking positions.

I do not mean to suggest that the social prestige of radio personalities or newspaper people is not high as well. However, the argument I am making is that, using the audience as a criterion, the status of television personalities is especially high. It is perhaps due to the visual aspects of television, the expected (and generally real) good looks of the interviewers, the glamor that is associated with it, and the heavy dependency that people have on television for their various needs. In any event, given this high status situation, there is also a high risk factor involved, should the interview not proceed well for whatever reason. In other words, television interviewers are more vulnerable if they fail; the higher up you are, the greater the fall can be.

What is true of the interviewer is also the case regarding the interviewee. There seems to be something about the television medium that has the potential of enhancing the status of people who appear on it. Although it has not been studied and "proven" by researchers in a direct and systematic manner, it can be assumed that if a person of relatively low social status is interviewed on television, his or her status in the eyes of colleagues, friends, and acquaintances, as well as by the general audience, could be enhanced significantly (assuming, of course, that the context of the interview was not of some negative act committed by the person). Something similar might occur if the person were interviewed in a radio program or by a newspaper, but probably to a lesser degree.

As for higher-status people such as politicians, experts, or high-ranking civil servants, a similar phenomenon can occur. However, there is also a greater risk factor because they are more vulnerable due to the greater exposure that the television medium provides as well as its visual properties. Thus if a politician blunders or an entertainer appears to be embarrassed during a television interview, the damage he or she will suffer might be greater than if the same thing occurred during a radio interview or appeared in the printed press. This is mainly because of the nature of the television medium and the fact that the viewers can notice the embarrassment more than in other media. And yet we must keep in mind that often the mishap can go unnoticed by most of the viewers and will become an issue only if and when someone (often a political opponent or a journalist) brings it to the attention of the public. In the latter case there might be less of a difference between television and other media. Recall, for example, President Ford's now famous slip of the tongue concerning Poland in the presidential debate several years ago.

What has just been suggested concerning the social status dimension is closely associated with the dimensions of the *publicity* and the *degree of confidentiality* of the interview. The television interview is by and large the most public of all forms of interviewing. This is due mainly to the combined audio and visual elements of the television medium as well as the relatively large audience that the medium attracts, all of which make the interview so vulnerable.

The dimension of the *accuracy of the interview protocol* is also more salient in television interviewing than in any other form of journalistic interviewing. It is relatively easy to edit a newspaper or radio interview without the readers or listeners being able to notice that excerpts were omitted from the full interview. In editing a television interview, however, it is virtually impossible to do so without leaving traces of the editing, especially for a sophisticated and experienced viewer. Thus despite special techniques that are used to cut out certain segments of the interview, this process is rarely left unnoticed.

As for the *social impact* on the interview, given the broad amplification of the mass media, and particularly of television, what is often said in a television interview, and how it is said, all can lead to a potentially enormous impact. Responsible interviewers and their interviewees are aware of this potential force of the interview, and presumably take this factor into consideration when they engage in the interviewing process.

As mentioned earlier, *time constraints* pose a special problem in television interviewing. Getting to a story and setting up the interview is logistically more complex in television than in any other medium. More equipment is needed to record the interview and to transmit it, both in live or in prerecorded formats. Also, television scheduling is very precise, more so than in any other mass medium (mainly in the United States). As a result, the timing of the interview, live or recorded, and the editing process must all be done with careful consideration of the program context in which the interview will be telecast. Despite what appears to be a tendency for shrinking news-holes in newspapers, it is likely that newspaper editors are still more flexible in deciding to allocate more space to a particular story if they deem this necessary. In the television industry, however, given the more severe constraints, comparable decisions are more complex and, therefore, less likely to be made.

Finally, the *location* and setting of the television interview is of special importance. The physical setting of the television interview is critical, since it can be seen by the viewers. Thus if an interview is conducted in an environment that is familiar to the interviewee, such as his or her home or place of work, even the background, decor, and artifacts in the room may influence the audience's perception of the interview (for example, the lit fire place, the national flag, the photograph of family members, the impressive library, and so on). Moreover, the presence of the director, floor manager, soundperson, and cameraperson, in addition to the bright shining lights, are all likely to influence the interviewee's behavior during the course of the interview and the impression that he or she makes on the audience. Thus these extra interviewing factors should be taken into account when discussing and analyzing the television interview.

CONCLUSION

This chapter has presented 12 dimensions according to which the journalistic interview can be compared with other professional nonjournalistic interviews. Using these dimensions, I have demonstrated that in certain respects the journalistic interview, including newspapers, radio, and television, differs from other forms of interviews, such as those between doctor and patient, lawyer and client, and researcher and respondent. The principal conclusion is that the journalistic interview is a highly dramatic encounter with numerous social, psychological, situational, and technological pressures operating on both the interviewer and the interviewee, and which are likely to affect in some ways the reader, listener, and viewer.

Following the explication of the dimensions, I indicated what seem to be the particular characteristics of the television interview among the different kinds of journalistic interviews. It was suggested that television interviews are even more problematic than those conducted for radio and newspapers particularly with regard to some of the dimensions.

2

THE TV INTERVIEW: ATTRIBUTES, FORMATS, AND CODES

Based on the function of the interview, its prominence in the program, the actual number of interviews and their duration, their degree of formality and the nature of the people who appear in them, a categorizing of television programs is created. A specification of the kinds of codes used in the subsequent analysis leads to identity codes, situational codes, verbal codes, and nonverbal codes.

In the previous chapter I described 12 dimensions that can be used to compare the journalistic interview with other kinds of interviews. Using those dimensions, we can determine how similar or how different the various forms of interviewing are. I also suggested that the television interview is a special form of journalistic interview. This chapter is devoted to a close and detailed look at the television interview.

The content of television consists of a wide variety of television programs, many of which contain interviewing. There are several different types of television interviews within these program formats. This large array of programs can be divided into several program formats using criteria that distinguish among various aspects of the interviewing situation. Thus there are several characteristics of the interview that can help classify interviewing on television and explain the different forms of television interviewing.

What are the attributes or characteristics of the television interview? How do they influence or shape program formats? And finally, what *codes* (or tools of analysis) are useful in explaining the television interview? This chapter tries to answer some of these questions.

The basic forms of the television repertoire that contain interviews are not unique to the United States. These forms exist in most Western countries with some variation. Thus the codes offered below can serve as tools for comparing and contrasting among different countries, as well as among networks and local and national programming. In later chapters these codes are used to compare the interviewing in the news on the three main American commercial networks (Chapter 4) and among four different countries (Chapter 5). The reader may wish, however, to use the codes to compare and contrast television interviewing in his or her home town, between commercial and public television stations, between specific programs, and so on.

ATTRIBUTES OF TELEVISION INTERVIEWING

A quick glance at any listing of television programming demonstrates the well-known fact that American television, in any particular community, presents numerous programs throughout the day. Some of these programs contain interviews while others do not. Thus in this context we are not concerned with movies, soap operas, action-adventure programs, musical variety shows, cartoons, and so on. We are also not interested in commercials, although some do contain interviewing. What we will examine is a wide variety of programs such as news programs, interview (talk) shows, panel discussions, public affairs programs, and the like. These programs not only contain interviews that are conducted and presented in various ways, but often are based solely on interviews.

In order to create a classification scheme it is necessary to develop criteria to distinguish among various elements of content, thereby assigning each element into a particular category. To classify television programs according to the way they use interviews requires some systematic analysis. The attributes are presented for clarity of sorting out the interview process. Naturally, some of them overlap and are not all mutually exclusive. They are presented to aid with an assessment of various kinds of interviews that exist on television, both in the United States and elsewhere. Following, then, are six attributes of the television interview in the framework of television programs.

The Function of the Interview

Broadly speaking, from the point of view of producers and audiences there are two main functions a television interview may serve in a television program: information and entertainment. Some interviews, such as those on news programs, are conducted mainly for information, while others, such as those on talk shows, are done mainly for entertainment. This does not mean to suggest, however, that no information can be presented or gained in an interview essentially conducted for entertainment, or that an interview conducted primarily for information cannot be entertaining. These latter situations can be considered as "blends" of information and entertainment.

The Prominence of the Interview

This attribute refers to the extent to which the interview is a prominent part of the program. In other words, it refers to the extent to which the program is devoted in its entirety to interviewing or whether it contains other things in addition to one or more interview. Thus, for example, the program can be devoted to one long interview; it could contain one or more shorter interviews; it could contain a variety of contents such as musical pieces, comedy acts, as well as one or more interviews; or it can consist of various news items, some or all of which contain interviews. The overall point is the extent to which the program contains little or much interviewing.

The Number of Interviews
and Interviewees

How many individual interviews are there in the program and how many individuals figure in the interview? Some programs contain only one interview while others contain two, three, or even numerous interviews. In some of the programs the different interviews are conducted separately, with one interviewee at a time, while in other programs all the interviewees are interviewed simultaneously.

The Length of the Interview

This attribute refers to the duration of the interview as it is presented on television. Some interviews in television programs are quite long, sometimes lasting as long as one hour or more. On the other hand, there are interviews which, as edited for airtime, last merely a few seconds. Thus there is much variability in terms of the duration of the interview.

The Formality of the Interview

This attribute is concerned with the degree of formality of the interview situations as it is presented on the screen. Some interviews are presented as being quite formal whereas other interviews are conducted in informal settings and are presented as such. Moreover, the degree of formality while the interview is conducted is not necessarily reflected in the way it is presented to the audience. Thus, for example, part of a formal (and perhaps lengthy) interview can be presented as a brief statement by the interviewee.

Homogeneity of Interviewee Types

This attribute refers to the kinds of people who appear in television interviews. Some programs that contain interviews are highly uniform, thus presenting interviews with only one kind of interviewee, for example, politicians, show business people, athletes, and so on. In other program formats the interviews are conducted with a variety of people; thus in the same program there can be politicians, show business people, and athletes. In the latter program format there might be on one occasion an interview with a politician, whereas on another occasion the interviewee might be a movie star. Moreover, if more than one interviewee appears in a single program, in some program formats all the interviewees would be of the same general kind (for instance, politicians or actors), whereas in other formats there can be a variety of people.

FORMATS OF INTERVIEWING
IN TELEVISION PROGRAMMING

Using an inductive approach, I shall now use these six attributes of television interviews to define and briefly describe several program formats common in television in the United States as well as in many other countries. What differentiates these formats from one another is the combination of their attributes and characteristics. The terms I have chosen to label these formats is arbitrary, of course, and should be considered within the purpose and framework of the present analysis. Some of these terms have been used elsewhere in the television literature, often ascribing similar meanings, but at times referring to somewhat different entities.

The way I define the program formats is by relating to different "profiles" based on the combinations of the attributes of television interviews explicated above. Using this scheme, it is possible to identify the profile of every program type in the television repertoire, or even label specific programs, as far as the interviewing contained in them is concerned.

Three points must be stressed, however. First, the attributes I have listed above are surely not the only ones that could be used to characterize the television interview. Other attributes, such as whether or not there is an audience present or whether or not it is broadcast live, could be used. I believe, however, that the attributes selected for this discussion are central in providing a general and relevant framework for the concept of the television interview. Second, obviously not all possible combinations of the six attributes and their respective elements actually exist. Thus it is futile even to attempt to talk about so many different kinds of television programs. Those selected for discussion here are the major ones of interest. And third, theoretically the three elements of each of the dimensions are mutually exclusive of one another, but in practice it often becomes difficult to ascertain precisely which profile fits each specific program within a program type. After all, it is common knowledge that within any program format there is some degree of variability as far as interviewing (or any other aspect of the program) is concerned. Thus, for example, within the category of "game shows" there are different specific shows, and within each show there may be some differences as far as interviewing is concerned. The same can be said of television news: There are different networks, different kinds of news shows (that is, national versus local, commercial versus public, and so on), and between any two newscasts there may be differences as well. The purpose, then, of the classification using the profiles is to provide a series of "ideal types" of the interview within the framework of the television program.

Below I present some examples of program types that contain interviewing. Figure 1 illustrates a summary of the six attributes labeled A through F, each with its respective elements. Derived from it are two examples of programs with interviews: game shows and national evening newscasts. A more detailed discussion follows.

Here, then, is a list of some of the kinds of interview-oriented program profiles that are possible: game shows, variety shows, talk shows, feature interviews, documentaries, current affairs, and news. Since the main concern of this book is with the news interviews, I shall begin with that format, but I will return to the other formats shortly by way of comparison.

News

Although I wish to deal with news as one format of television programming, it seems that I must present four subcategories, each with its distinctive interview profile.

The first of these formats of television news is usually referred to as national evening network news (ABC's *World News Tonight,* CBS's *Evening News* and NBC's *Nightly News*). The interviewing profile in this kind of news program is $A_1B_1C_3D_1E_1F_3$, which indicates that the interviews are informative in nature; that they constitute a small part of the newscast; that there are numerous interviews in a given newscast; that they are brief in duration; that they are almost always conducted in a formal setting; and that the interviewees are various people from all walks of life, although many are politicians, experts, and the like.

The second format of television news includes such programs as the *MacNeil/Lehrer NewsHour,* which is carried by the Public Broadcasting stations. This program's interviewing profile is somewhat

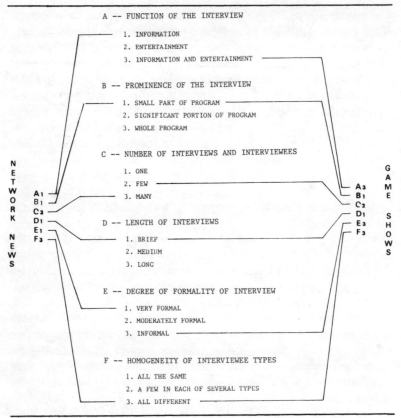

Figure 1   Examples of Television Program Profiles Containing Interviews

different: $A_1B_2C_2D_2E_1F_3$. Thus this particular news program involves informational interviews; the interviewing takes up a large proportion of the newscast; there are few interviewees in each newscast; they are relatively long in duration; they are very formal; and various kinds of people appear on it, although mostly they are politicians, experts, and so on.

The third category of news programs is that of the morning news magazines, which are broadcast nationally by the commercial networks (ABC's *Good Morning America,* CBS's *Morning News* and NBC's *Today Show*). This program structure essentially contains two subprograms, each with its characteristic interviews. The first is a miniature newscast, presented by a news anchorperson and is similar in general terms to the national evening news format, except for the fact that it lasts about five to seven minutes, and is repeated with some variation four times during the two-hour program. The profile of this segment is thus the same as for the national evening news format. (As I write this, the decision to change the format of the CBS *Morning News* has been made; it will be interesting to see if and how the interviewing format in the alternate program will be modified.)

The other subprogram, which is similar to the television "talk show," is conducted by the "hosts" of the program (traditionally a male and a female). The interview profile of this segment is different, however: $A_3B_2C_2D_2E_2F_3$. This indicates that the interviews are done both for information and entertainment; the interviews take up a significant portion of the program; there are several interviewees on each program; they are medium in duration; they are moderately formal; and the interviewees are various kinds of people.

The fourth and final category of television news, based on the classification of the interviews contained in them, is that of local news programs produced by the network affiliated stations as well as by independent stations. Given the fact that there are so many local stations and newscasts, any attempt to provide a single profile might be somewhat misleading. In any event, the following $A_3B_1C_3D_1E_2F_3$ profile is fairly representative of this format of television programming. Thus interviews on the local news programs are information as well as entertainment oriented; they constitute only a small part of the newscast; there are fairly numerous interviews in each newscast; they are brief in duration; they are moderately formal (although there are some very formal and some very informal ones); and many kinds of people appear as interviewees.

Game Shows

In contrast to news programs, it may seem at first glance that game shows do not belong in this analysis since they have no interviewing at all. And yet, it seems reasonable to consider as interviews the brief segments of such programs in which the host or master of ceremony introduces the contestants and asks them questions such as where they come from, what they do for a living, what they are doing in Los Angeles (where most of these shows are produced), and so on. Thus I would define game shows such as *Name That Tune, Family Feud,* and *Tic Tac Dough* as programs with a $A_3B_1C_2D_1E_3F_3$ profile.

Translating this symbolic profile into prose, we might say that the game show is typically one in which the function of the interviewing is to provide information as well as entertainment. In addition, interviewing usually takes up a very small part of the program and there are typically several contestants or participants (interviewees) in a given show. Moreover, the interviews are usually brief, often consisting of two or three very short questions and answers, the interview is very informal, and finally, the contestants being interviewed usually have varied backgrounds and are, thus, of different types.

Variety Shows

Another form of television program is the variety show such as the *Tonight Show with Johnny Carson* or the *David Letterman Show,* which usually consists of a few interviews as well as some entertainment segments, sometimes performed by the same people who are interviewed and sometimes by other people. Using our interview classification scheme, this kind of program would be characterized as having a $A_2B_2C_2D_2E_3F_2$ profile. In other words, variety shows usually contain interviews that are intended to entertain, rather than provide information; they take up a considerable part of the time of the program; there usually are a few such interviews in the program; the interviews are medium in length, lasting several minutes each; they are conducted in an informal manner; and the "guests" on the shows (as the interviewees are referred to) are usually of various types—singers, actors, and so on.

Talk Shows

This format of television programming, including programs such as the *Phil Donahue Show* or *Firing Line,* essentially consists of several interviews with a variety of people. Its interview profile would be $A_1B_3C_2D_3E_2F_3$. Thus the talk show format involves interviews primarily intended to provide information; the interviews take up the entire program; there usually are several personalities being interviewed in a given program; the interviews are relatively long; they are done in what would be considered as a moderately formal way; and the interviewees are of various types (politicians, professionals, artists, and the like).

Feature Interviews

This television program format is one that I suggest is only slightly different from the previous kind, differing on only one of the six attributes, that of the degree of formality of the interview. Thus the profile of the feature interview would be $A_1B_3C_2D_3E_1F_3$. This kind of interview program, such as the *Barbara Walters Special,* is mainly for information; the interviews take up the whole time slot of the program; there are usually two or three interviews in the program (although in this category one could conceivably think of an entire program devoted to one interview as used to be the case on the *Dick Cavett Show*); they are long in duration; they are formal; and the interviewees are of various types.

Documentaries

This program format includes such programs as *60 Minutes* and *20/20*. Its profile with respect to the interviewing it contains is $A_1B_2C_3D_2E_2F_3$. Thus the interviewing in documentary programs is aimed at providing information; the interviews take up a significant portion of the program; there usually are several people interviewed in each report (the program often deals with more than one report but could conceivably be devoted to only one report); the interviews are of medium length; they are moderately formal (although sometimes they might be characterized as very formal); and people of various types would be interviewed.

Current Affairs

The category of current affairs programs consists of programs such as *Face the Nation, Meet the Press, This Week with David Brinkley* and *Nightline.* However, I would suggest that slightly different profiles should be presented here for the various programs. Thus *Face the Nation* and *Meet the Press* are very similar and would be characterized as having a $A_1B_3C_1D_3E_1F_1$ profile. In these programs, the objective is to provide information; the interview takes up the whole program; there is one interviewee; it is long; it is very formal; and the interviewees are usually always politicians, that is, of one type, although there sometimes are exceptions.

As for *This Week with David Brinkley,* the profile would probably look like $A_1B_2C_1D_3E_1F_1$. This indicates that the program is also for informational purposes; a significant part of the program is devoted to interviewing; there usually is only one "guest" interviewee (if excluding consideration of the special form of interviewing in which Mr. Brinkley "interviews" his own reporter colleagues, usually toward the end of the program); the interview is quite long; it is quite formal; and the interviewees are usually of the same category, namely, politicians. Thus this program differs from the earlier two in the current affairs format mainly with respect to the part of the entire program taken up by the interview and related to this, the length of the interview.

Nightline presents another version in this general category. Thus it has a $A_1B_2C_2D_2E_2F_2$ profile. Putting this into words, *Nightline* is also for information purposes; a significant part of the program is devoted to the interviews; there are usually several interviewees, some in the filmed report that usually starts the program going and some in the direct interviews that follow; the interviews are usually of medium length, but in the filmed report they are often shorter; the degree of formality is moderate, especially given Ted Koppel's idiosyncratic style; and the interviewees are usually of several types—politicians, experts of various kinds, and so on.

This current affairs format category clearly demonstrates the versatility of the classification scheme used. Whereas in the game shows, the variety shows, the talk shows, the feature interviewing, and the documentary programs, most of the respective examples that can be given are highly similar, the current affairs category indicates some variation. This poses a conceptual dilemma: Should the category list of program formats be expanded, thereby giving some television programs a category of their own (clearly some program producers would believe that their programs deserve such a position), or should we use the flexibility of the profile notation system to allow for slight differences within a given category? I have chosen the latter option, although the reader may wish to use the former approach. In any event, the use of the profiling scheme allows for flexibility among programs while pointing out the general rules as well as the inevitable exceptions.

In sum, it is suggested that in examining television interviews using the six attributes there appear to be several program formats that differ in terms of the role of interviewing in them. Moreover, while the six latter program formats I presented are fairly similar in most Western countries, interviewing in television news is quite different in the various countries. Much of the discussion ahead will focus on these differences and will attempt to explain them.

THE CODES OF TELEVISION INTERVIEWING

As noted earlier, the major premise here is that the television interview is a dramatic and potentially problematic encounter. It entails complex technological and logistic operations and involves salient social and psychological factors. It is a dynamic process of communication that is highly demanding of its participants.

At this point I wish to enumerate and describe several codes that operate in the course of television interviewing. What I mean by a "code" is a characteristic of some sort that can be employed to compare different interviews systematically, either within the same program format (interview profile) or among program formats, within a given country or across countries, as well as within a particular point in time or over time. In other words, a code should be conceived of as a variable for which empirical data can be gathered. As with any variable, each code must have at least two possible entities or values. A special way of looking at the code is the analysis of whether the particular feature is present or absent.

Later in the text a comparison will be made of the way interviews are conducted in television news on the three commercial American networks and how the interview is used in the major television news broadcasts of several other countries. Thus we need to become familiar with the codes, a process that will become truly meaningful when these comparisons are made. It should already be clear that on some of the codes there will be little if any variability among ABC, CBS, and NBC, whereas for others there might be large differences. The differences will become even more meaningful when we do the cross-cultural comparison.

Four major categories of codes are relevant to the analysis and understanding of television interviewing: identity codes, situational codes, verbal codes, and nonverbal codes. It will soon become clear that some of the codes are unique to television interviewing, while others could be considered as relevant to other journalistic interviewing, and in some cases to nonjournalistic interviewing as well.

IDENTITY CODES

Of the four major code categories, the identity codes are the least unique to television. The identity codes refer to the "inherent" characteristics of the person being interviewed. They are important since they may be consequential in determining how the interview will be done and how it will proceed. The identity codes presented below do not totally exhaust all the possible characteristics of the interviewee. They are sufficient, however, to characterize each interviewee in a manner that will be relevant to the course the interview might take and for the purpose of making comparisons between different interviews. Furthermore, it should be noted that all the codes are relevant for each interviewee. Three groups of identity codes are specified.

Demographic Characteristics

The first group consists of two demographic characteristics: *gender* and *place of origin*. Whether the interviewee is male or female has potential significance in that it can speak to the question of the equality or inequality of women and men in society and in the variety of roles they fulfill. Also, whether or not the interviewee is native to the place of origin of the broadcast can be important, as it might indicate the extent to which the news is parochial or cosmopolitan. In this respect one can deal with the national or local level, that is, whether the interviewee is an American or a foreigner (from the point of view of the U.S. networks), or whether he or she is a New Yorker, for example, from the point of view of WCBS, WABC or WINS in New York.

Role in Society

A second group of identity codes is concerned with the role of the interviewee in society. Specifically, we are interested in three character-istics: whether or not the interviewee is a *public official* (for example, a civil servant, a judge, and so on); whether or not the interviewee is a *professional or expert* in some particular field (for instance, a doctor, a scientist, an economist, and the like); and whether or not the interviewee was *elected* to his or her position (for instance, a mayor of a town or the President of the United States). These three characteristics will enable us to determine if the interviewee is a relatively high-ranking person or not.

Relationship to the Story

The third and final group of identity codes deals with the relationship the interviewee has to the story being reported (this group of codes is generally more pertinent to programs on public affairs and news). The first code in this class is whether or not the interviewee is a *random* or nonrandom choice. Thus, for example, if any striking worker on the picket line is interviewed concerning the reasons for the strike, that choice would be considered as *random* since any other member could have been approached and interviewed. If, however, the interview is with the head of the union local, then the choice of that individual would be a *nonrandom* one.

The second code here is whether or not the person being interviewed is *involved* in the issue being discussed. Thus, for example, if a passerby is interviewed about what caused a traffic accident, that person would be considered as *not* involved in the story. However, if the interview is conducted with the driver of one of the vehicles, that choice would be considered as selecting a person who is definitely *involved* in the story.

The final code in this group is whether or not the interviewee is a *victim* (note that being involved may or may not be equivalent to being a victim). Thus, for example, if a person whose house has just burned down is interviewed, that person would be characterized as a victim, whereas the fireman on the scene would not be a victim, although the latter is clearly involved in the story being reported.

SITUATIONAL CODES

Situational codes are usually unique to broadcast interviews, both radio and television. In this category I include three groups of codes: the *location* of the interview, the *directness of the broadcast,* and *editing.* These three groups deal with particular aspects of the situation in which the interview takes place and the way it is presented to the audience.

The Location of the
Television Interview

The first point in the location codes is *where* the interview takes place. The major distinction is between *studio* and *on-location* interviews. From our perspective, there are two main kinds of studio setting: news studios and nonnews studios. As for the on-location setting, there are several varieties, such as indoor versus out-of-doors; public versus private places; home versus place of work; and so on. The second point refers to the extent to which the interview is conducted *face-to-face* or by means of a *remote* arrangement. In other words, do the participants sit (or stand) facing one another, or are they only connected via some electronic hook-up such as microwave, satellite, or simply by means of a telephone. The latter situation can vary from another studio in the same building to a complex circuit linking an astronaut in outer space with an interviewer on the ground. The location of the interview is important, as it can have a strong impact on how the interview proceeds. When both parties are in the studio, the interviewer has the "home" advantage. When the interview is conducted on-location, the interviewee may be more familiar with the setting and thus have an advantage. Generally the studio interview guarantees a more quiet and respectable setting, whereas the interview "on location" can often be awkward, embarrassing, and at times even dangerous. In face-to-face interviews both parties can utilize interpersonal feedback cues, whereas in remote arrangements the interviewer often has the advantage in being able to see the interviewee, but the interviewee can only hear the interviewer but not see him or her.

The Directness of the
Broadcast of the Interview

Live television interviews have taken place since the early days of the medium. The context was different, however, from what it is today. When the television era began, most programs were presented "live" from the television studio, since there were no technological means to prerecord them. The only exception was the use of film when feature movies and newsreels were shown. As a matter of fact, newsreels required developing and transporting the film to the studio, which could be far away, and therefore proved time consuming. With the advent of videotape (and later of microwave technologies) it became possible to record interviews (as well as other programs) for broadcast at some other point in time or to transmit them "live" from another (often distant) location. Thus today's television interview can be rerecorded or presented "live" from virtually any location.

The main advantage of the "live" interview is that it takes place in "real time." This is particularly important when time is of essence, mainly in news and current affairs reporting. The main advantage of the prerecorded interview is that if something in the interaction went wrong (on the part of the interviewer, the interviewee or both, as well as some external problem) the interview can be done over and be presented to the audience as a "better" product. Also, the taped interview can be used when interviewing takes place over varying time zones or when the interview can only be obtained at a time other than the scheduled program.

Editing

The final code to be discussed is that of *editing*. An interview can be presented in full, that is, the way it was conducted, or it can be edited. The editing possibility exists, of course, only for interviews that are taped prior to their being telecast. Editing can take many forms ranging from brief deletions in order to shorten the interview or the removal of some specific segment, to drastic editing in which only a few words from an interviewee's reply are kept and presented as a "sound bite," without the audience even hearing the question posed by the interviewer.

The use, form, and extent of editing depends upon the nature of the program, the time constraints available, and the prior understanding between the interviewer and the interviewee. Editing always runs the risk of modifying the meaning and context of what was said in the interview and the information that is presented to the audience. Editing is important not only in making the interview fit the time constraints of the program, but also in highlighting and emphasizing certain points that the interviewer wishes to make salient.

VERBAL CODES

The verbal codes presented here are also not inherently related to television interviewing, although sometimes some of them may be manifested in a special way in the television context. This is mainly because all interviewing involves verbal interaction, which essentially means that questions are asked and answers are given. There are two groups of verbal codes: *questioning techniques* and *rules of etiquette*.

Questioning Techniques

The essence of a good interview is asking the correct question, which will elicit the appropriate reply. There are various kinds of questions and ways of stating them to the interviewee. Questions can be "neutral" or "indirect," which suggest to the interviewee and the audience that the interviewer is not biased, that is, has no personal position and advocates no particular preference. On the other hand, there are "loaded" or "direct" questions that clearly indicate to the interviewee and the audience that the interviewer is attempting to pressure or to "corner" the interviewee. The term *provocative questions* is used for this kind of approach to the interviewee.

Thus, for example, in an interview with a top-ranking politician, the interviewer who may think that the politician should resign might ask: "What do you think you should do given what has happened?" or he or she might say: "Don't you think that given what has happened you should resign?" The former approach is a neutral question whereas the latter is a provocative question.

Questions also vary in terms of whether or not they are *planned in advance* by the interviewer. In most journalistic interviews there is some plan that the interviewer develops prior to the interview. Accordingly, the interviewer knows ahead of time some of the questions that he or she will ask during the interview. However, many questions depend on the answers given by the interviewee to previous questions. Thus the "follow-up" questions require an exact formulation during the course of the interview, and cannot generally appear in the list of questions that the interviewer prepares in advance.

The use of the different kinds of questions by the interviewer sets the stage for the interview itself. The way the questions are formulated will determine to a large extent the amount and quality of the information that will be obtained. Also, the way the questions are asked is an important factor in the form of interaction that will ensue during the course of the interview.

Rules of Etiquette

The term "etiquette" means various things in the course of the interview, all of which are important in the way the interview commences, proceeds, and ends. The way the interviewee is *introduced* and is *referred to* is important in establishing the relationship that will develop during the course of the interview. Are official titles such as "Mr. President" or "Senator" used, or are last names, or possibly even first names used? Moreover, is there a reciprocal relationship or is it a one-sided arrangement? Thus, for example, if Ted Kennedy is approached in an interview as "Senator Kennedy," does Kennedy refer to the interviewer as "Mr. Brokaw" or "Tom"?

In this connection, what impression is created in the interview? Is the interviewee speaking to the interviewer or to the television audience? For example, a reply could begin with the phrase: "Well, *Mr Y*, I think . . . ," or, "Well, *Ted,* I think . . ." Both these cases indicate a response directed at the interviewer. On the other hand, the reply could be: "Well, I think . . . ," which does not contain the direct reference to the interviewer. The difference may initially seem to be insignificant or trivial, but it is believed that the former approach, interjecting the name of the interviewer, is part of the "performance" or the "staging" of the interview as an interpersonal encounter, and is typical of certain kinds of interviews and not of others.

Another aspect of the rules of etiquette has to do with *interrupting* the interviewees or allowing them to complete what they are saying before the interviewer moves on to another question. Interviews vary on this factor to a large extent. Thus sometimes the interviewee is interrupted often, and is given little chance to express his or her opinion, whereas on other occasions the interviewee is given the opportunity to reply at length and in detail. This seems to be the case regardless of whether or not the interview will be edited, which seems to suggest that this is a stylistic point rather than one of interviewer strategy. Related to the latter point is the extent to which the interviewer tries to force the interviewee to be brief by saying something such as "please state this briefly" or "we're running out of time, so please be brief."

The next verbal code is *verbal feedback*. Feedback is provided by the interviewer to the interviewee in the form of such expressions as "aha," "yes," "I see," and so on. This feedback can serve as reinforcement to what the interviewee is saying, both in terms of encouraging the interviewee to continue talking, and sometimes in the sense of indicating agreement to what he or she is saying.

The final element in the verbal category, (although some might consider this as belonging in the category of nonverbal codes), is the use of voice intonation. The interviewer can use his or her voice to indicate agreement, but more often disagreement, disbelief, or doubt. The use of voice intonation is sometimes purposive and at times unconscious, but the extent to which it is used can have an impact on the course of the interaction taking place.

NONVERBAL CODES

Whereas the identity and verbal codes were not unique to television, the nonverbal codes are indeed quite unique to the television medium. In other words, the information one can obtain by means of a television interview is both verbal and nonverbal. This major coding category will include three specific groups of nonverbal codes: *spatial* codes, *artifactual codes,* and *filmic* codes.

Spatial Codes

Spatial codes refer to the way space is used in the interaction between the interviewer and the interviewee. Using Edward Hall's notion of varying distances, we may consider four possibilities. The "intimate" distance is very small (several inches) and typically occurs when the interview is conducted in a crowded setting such as an airport lounge or in the downtown section of a large city. In such a situation the participants might almost be touching one another. The "personal" distance, that of several feet, can be, for example, when the participants sit at right angles to each other or on either side of a table. The studio interview is often set up in such a way that several yards separate the interviewer and the interviewee, which would be an example of the "social" distance. Finally, the "public" distance is the greatest, such as when a reporter in an auditorium stands up and asks the president a question at a press conference (I mention this type even though we have not gone into detail about press conferences). Of course all these situations refer to face-to-face interviews, whereas sometimes the participants are many miles apart, hooked up via satellite. This physical proximity factor is important for the way the interview is conducted, since the distance can have an effect on the power relationships as well as on the ability of the interviewee to "protect" himself or herself from the interviewer. The *setting* of the television studio designed for an interview can be arranged in various ways. Thus, for example, the interviewee and the interviewer can be seated in similar chairs or in different ones, they can be seated facing each other or at right angles to each other, and there may or may not be some object of furniture separating them, such as a table, a desk, or a rostrum. These factors serve an important role in establishing the "relationship" between the interviewer and the inter-viewee. Another aspect of the proximity arrangements is whether or not the participants have *eye contact* with each other. Not facing each other, being too close or too far, or being in other locations such as in another studio, can make a difference in terms of how the two persons relate to one another. Visual feedback from either party, including head nods, smiles, or the raising of eyebrows can be useful or detrimental. But in any event, they must be visible.

Artifactual Codes

The second kind of nonverbal codes are the artifactual codes. What I mean by artifactual codes is the presence or use of various kinds of artifacts during the course of the interview. Interviews conducted outside the studio can be set up in a variety of ways: The interviewee may be seated in an office, behind a desk with a bookcase in the background, the interview may be conducted in a garden amidst colorful flowers; it may be conducted at the entrance to a factory where workers are on strike carrying picket signs; or the interview may be done in a crowded air terminal with many people rushing by as the backdrop. Whatever the setting, it is assumed that it will have some impact on the atmosphere in which the interview is conducted, and on the effects it may have on the viewers.

The use of objects in the presentation of information is another artifactual code. In many interviews there is no use of such objects; however, when experts of various kinds are interviewed, such as scientists or artists, it is not uncommon to see interviewees such as experts using objects such as maps, tables, graphs, and physical models of the subject being discussed in order to demonstrate what is being said.

The use of *microphones* in a television interview is self-evident. However, there are various ways in which microphones are used, and they may have an influence on the form of the interaction taking place. Thus, for example, a miniature lavalier microphone might be fastened to each of the participants, making them relatively unobtrusive. This is typically done in studio settings. Another possibility in the studio is the use of desk microphones. In both cases, the interviewee and the interviewer have their own microphones and can thus speak and be heard whenever they please.

The use of technician-operated microphones such as the overhead "boom" or the below the frame "shotgun" are other possibilities (the former is more common in the studio and the latter on location). These microphones can be quite obtrusive from the interviewee's point of view, particularly if he or she lacks experience in such a role.

Finally, there is the hand-held microphone used by many reporters. This kind of microphone gives the interviewer a leading advantage in that he or she can "permit" the interviewee to speak, by pointing the microphone in his or her direction, or what is more important, the interviewer can "prevent" the interviewee from speaking by taking the microphone away. This can create an added aspect to the drama of the interaction. It should be mentioned that in an interview recorded "on location" sometimes the interviewer does not even use a microphone when asking the questions. Back in the studio, during the editing process, the questions can be inserted, if necessary.

Filmic Codes

Filmic codes refer to the shots and techniques used by the camera people in filming and framing the interview. The first kind of shot is one that provides the setting of the interview, that is, the establishing shot. This frame generally shows the interviewer and the interviewee together, thus providing the spatial and contextual relationship between them. Sometimes it only gives the interviewee in a wider frame so that the audience can see where the interview is taking place. Thus in interviews done "on location" the establishing shot will provide important information as to where and under what circumstances the interview is being conducted. The establishing shot is particularly important, however, when the participants are not in a face-to-face situation, so that the viewer can get the correct perspective of the situation.

Since an interview involves at least two participants, the use of cuts, that is, the changing of the frame from one person to the other by means of switching from one camera to another (or editing the interview to give such an appearance) is important for the flow of the interview. It allows the person speaking to be seen, or for a reaction shot of the person listening. The rate of camera switching could be an indication of the degree of verbal exchange between the participants, and could imply something about the dramatic nature of the encounter.

The *size of the image* on the television screen is another filmic code. Thus the use of frames in which the person talking (most often the interviewee) is seen very close up, with his or her face (and sometimes only portions of it) taking up the entire screen, is a highly dramatic shot. The "close-up" is used to concentrate on facial features of the interviewee and often gives the impression of the camera "invading" the privacy of the person. It should be noted that an extreme close-up shot presents an "abnormal" frame, from the point of view of the face-to-face interaction. In fact, it is physically impossible for a person to come up close enough to another person so that only the chin, mouth, nose, and eyes make up the entire frame and are still in focus. Only a camera can present such an extreme "intimate" picture of a person. In television interviewing the use of the close-up shot is often associated with embarrassing questions or in situations where there is some doubt as to the veracity of the reply being given.

The close-up of the interviewee can be obtained in two ways, either by a direct cut from a "medium" shot or by zooming in, whereby the camera gradually narrows in on the face of the interviewee. The latter is generally perceived to be more dramatic in that the interviewee is perceived to be slowly locked in and captured by the interviewer.

Reaction shots are pictures taken of the person not speaking at a given point in time. Sometimes the reaction shot is of the interviewer listening to the interviewee, and sometimes the interviewee is shown as he or she is listening to the question being posed by the interviewer. In the latter case, the viewer can see the facial reactions of the interviewee as he or she hears the question and plans to reply. A special kind of reaction shot is used in situations were there is more than one interviewee, such as in a debate, in which case the camera may show one interviewee while another is speaking. Reaction shots quite often reveal the attitude that the listener has toward the person speaking. Sometimes reaction shots show both interviewer and interviewee by means of a split screen.

The final filmic code is a special kind of reaction shot, namely, a shot of some part of the interviewee's body other than the face, usually the hands. Sometimes the camera focuses on trembling fingers or on clasped hands. These behaviors are often considered as revealing tension on the part of the person speaking, thus the camera brings them along with the speaker's face.

CONCLUSION

This chapter proposed a classification of the formats of television interviews. Six attributes, according to which we can distinguish among different kinds of television programs containing interviews, were proposed: the function of the interview, the salience of the interview, the frequency of interviews and interviewees, the duration of the interviews, the formality of the interviews, and the degree of homogeneity of interviewee types. Using these attributes several program formats were presented, including several varieties of television news.

Also presented were four major categories of codes according to which we can analyze the television interview: identity codes, verbal codes, nonverbal codes, and situational codes. We described some of the components of each of these codes, and suggested that they may be useful in comparing interviews across networks, countries, and points in time. This will be done later in the book, with special emphasis on the television news interview.

3

MANUAL OF MANUALS:
RULES OF THE GAME

What does the professional literature have to say about television news interviews and how they should be conducted? Not terribly much. The prescriptions for good interviewing are reviewed and summarized using the coding scheme previously developed.

The literature of journalism and mass communication is replete with images of interviews ranging from Lincoln Steffen's interview with Lenin, which gave the vigorous muckraker a glimpse of post-Revolutionary Russia to others that offered insights on presidents, premiers, and other significant people. What has been written about the journalistic interview ranges from historical articles about the origins of the interview to sociological studies about how various journalists do their work.

However, most of what has been written about interviews and interviewing is in textbooks and reporting manuals. While useful, much of this material is based on the personal experience of the author with reference to what other journalists have done in given situations. What this work lacks is any systematic approach. The student reading such material doesn't know whether the interviewing practices being presented are typical or unusual. Moreover, there is little specificity about how a given interview was done, under what circumstances and with what "intellectual equipment" by the interviewer. Some of this kind of information can be gleaned from the anecdotal examples of great interviewers who have written books detailing their experiences—such as Barbara Walters, Oriana Fallaci, and Mike Wallace—but even those valuable insights are the view of one person what may or may not be generalized for use by others.

Moreover, even textbooks devoted to news reports do not give the news interview much attention. Although some of the texts devote an entire chapter to this topic, others provide only several pages or even a mere few paragraphs. This is despite the fact that the interview is one of the most central tools that the television journalist uses in gathering information and presenting it in the newscast.

As stated, the remainder of this book is devoted to interviewing in the news and not to other types of programs in which interviewing takes place. Also, I shall restrict the discussion to interviewing conducted by reporters in the studio and on location, with the exclusion of news conferences. News conferences will not be covered here, although they may be considered a special form of interview. I have avoided dealing with news conferences for several specific reasons: First, what typifies the news conferences is the fact that there are several, and often numerous, reporters who attempt to ask their question while the person holding the news conference, or a press agent or public relations person, recognizes the various reporters and allows them to ask their respective questions; second, moreover, the news conference often begins with a "statement" by the speaker; and third, the news conference is often referred to in the literature as a "pseudoevent," in which case the questions and answers are not part of a genuine interview, but rather part of the "staging" of the event. Incidentally, it is sometimes difficult for the television news viewer, using the cues provided in the interview clip itself, to determine whether or not the person being interviewed was speaking at a news conference or in a bona fide interview.

THE LITERATURE

Numerous books and articles have been written on the general topic of interviewing. Some of this literature is of a practical nature in the form of manuals and textbooks, and some (mainly in article form) is based on research. Also, there is a significant body of literature in the field of *journalism* that mentions the interview in one way or another. This literature consists of several books devoted to journalistic interviewing, including those by Anderson and Benjaminson (1976), Metzler (1977), Mollenhoff (1981), and Biagi (1986). These books cover various issues, such as how to prepare reporters for good interviewing and the use of the interview in creating good impressions by executives.

As for specific literature on the television *news* interview, surprisingly little is available. The following references all have in common the fact that they deal specifically with television news interviewing, and do not simply mention the television interview in the more general context of news gathering. Most of them can be characterized as "cook books" that focus on various practical aspects of television news. Moreover, they do cover, in some fashion, some of the variables that are relevant in analyzing the television news interview and that I have explicated above. Thus they will serve as the point of departure for looking into how journalists are told what the television news interview *ought* to be. These sources are not what we consider today as critical analysts of television news (for example, Conrad, 1982; Newcomb, 1982), a branch of the literature gaining popularity that also makes reference, at times, to television news interviewing (for example, Hartley, 1982).

In chronological order, the texts covered here are: Green (1969), Dary (1971), Fang (1972), Siller (1972), Tyrrell (1972), Gelles (1974), Davis (1976), Metzler (1977), Yorke (1978), Shook (1982), Lewis (1984), and Biagi (1986). Clearly, these are not the only sources available, but they should suffice in giving us a clear notion of what the literature says. It is also interesting that many of these sources are from the early 1970s, at a time when the concept of television news was being shaped in the general way as it is today.

The first point one notes when examining these publications is the large degree of overlap between the various authors in terms of the relatively few topics and issues they discuss and the apparent consensus concerning the actual views and perceptions of what makes for good television news interviewing. Notable, also, are the issues which most, and at times all of the authors, completely disregard, including issues such as the topics best suited for interviewing, the way interviewees are selected, the selection of the interview sites and artifacts used in the interview, some of the nonverbal characteristics of the interview (with the exception of the camera shots), and most of the social and psychological antecedents, constraints, and possible effects that interviews might have on the viewing public.

In the following brief review I shall mention and discuss those topics covered in the references cited. I do not wish to elaborate at this point on what the various authors fail to mention. This I shall do later. In the remainder of this chapter I shall present the different topics and describe what the authors say about them, using the general order of the concepts presented in Chapter 2, namely, beginning with the identity codes, followed by the situational codes, continuing with the verbal codes and culminating with nonverbal codes.

GENERAL PREPARATION
AND CONTROL

There are two different, yet related, general notions that seem to permeate much of the literature. These are preparations and control. They are relevant to the discussion of various aspects of the television news interview, as well as concerning other kinds of interviews.

Preparing for the interview is a central point raised by many of the authors. Preparation is important mainly with regard to the verbal aspects of the interview. This is particularly salient in the discussion concerning the interviewer's need to learn and become familiar with the topic of the interview, the formulation of the questions that the interviewer plans to ask the respondent, and the way the interviewer is supposed to approach the interviewee prior to and during the interview. Virtually every textbook examined stressed some of these aspects of the preparation for the interview.

As for control, the literature devotes relatively much space and importance to this general concept. Thus, for example, Lewis (1984) states in unequivocal terms:

> The control of the interview should rest in the reporter's hands. If the subject gains the upper hand, it become a farce [p. 124].

Dary (1971) made the point in a less dramatic fashion by saying,

> The purpose of any interview is to gain information. . . . But since the newsman has little control over his subject, he must do as much as he can to control the interview [p. 78]

Two writers talk of the control factor using "military" terminology. Thus Gelles (1974) says,

> A key aspect in the construction of television interview reality is the reporter's ability to *seize* control of the interaction at its start and maintain it through the filming [p. 39; my emphasis].

Also, in the Bolch and Miller (1978) volume on investigative reporting (which does not specifically deal with television and was, therefore, not cited earlier), the title of the chapter on interviewing is "Drafting the Battle Plan: Controlling the Interview" (p. 59).

Metzler (1977) cites a professor of broadcasting who lists several problems with the interview. One of them is the "frequently successful effort by public figures to control the interview" (p. 99). Of course, the interviewer is warned about this and suggestions are made on how to overcome the problem. Shook (1982), for example, offers some specific pieces of advice, among them:

> Some interviewees will talk nonstop. . . . When such people stop to breathe, be ready to jump in with a new question. In normal conversation,

such an interruption might be considered rude. On television, the game interruption may be barely noticeable to home viewers [p. 68].

IDENTITY CODES

The notions of preparation and control are closely associated with the identity codes of the television news interview. Who is assigned to cover what particular story and to conduct which specific interview are issues that news editors and producers constantly need to come to grips with. Moreover, the question of who is going to be interviewed is a poignant issue. However, since the literature does not distinguish in this context among the three kinds of identity codes I have proposed, I shall present the available references concerning all three (demographic characteristics, roles in society, and relationship to the story) in a combined fashion.

One of the specific means for controlling the interview is the way the interviewer selects the interviewees he or she wishes to interview. In very broad terms, we can mention two kinds of interviewees: "elite" persons such as politicians and other leading persons in business, science, and other fields; and the "man in the street." Biagi (1986) talks about essentially the same classification when she refers to the interviewees as "public figures" and "private citizens." What is more important, however, according to Biagi, is that the interviewee is a person for whom one or more of the following is important: their job, their accomplishments, the crime with which they are charged, what or whom they know, what they have seen, what has happened to them, or the trend they represent.

The interviewer generally seeks to speak with the person in the news, the one responsible for the facts of the story being reported, and not with just "anyone." And yet, the interviewer quite often must exercise some degree of selectivity, as there may be more people involved that he or she can deal with at the same time. Thus the selection process is related to the degree of control the interviewer wishes to maintain. Interviewers know how the various personalities "behave" during an interview, and they know that public figures generally want to appear on the screen. As Lewis (1984) notes,

Often the public figure is delighted to be asked. He is probably flattered that you thought of him, and glad of the chance to be seen and heard on television [pp. 119-120].

The situation with regard to the "man in the street" interview is not all that random either, according to Gelles (1974). He claims,

> Rather than randomly choosing people from a crowd, the reporter selects people he knows personally. . . . The selection is also tempered by the potential subject's social characteristics. The reporter seeks a balance . . . in terms of points of view, age, sex and color. The reporter is also concerned with selecting respondents who will not violate the norms of a television interview. They cannot use obscenities, speak on the wrong topic, mumble, appear to be nervous, or perform in such a way that the section of film will be useless for broadcast [p. 40].

SITUATIONAL CODES

Activities in the context of the second category of codes, that of situational codes, also have an important bearing on the preparation for, and the control of, the television news interview.

Location of the Interview

The physical location of the interview is an important and salient point in some of the literature. As Green (1969) observed long ago:

> The difficulty with the film interview lies in its lack of movement; it is pictorially static. Its strength is in its content. . . . Where a choice of location is possible, the choice may be to improve the visual quality of the interview. But the choice must be made in relation to the content [p. 170].

Yorke (1978) also comments along these lines:

> Far more desirable from the reporter's point of view is the selection of a background appropriate to the particular story. It makes far more sense to interview the scientist in the laboratory rather than in front of a plain office wall, to talk to the newspaper editor against the background of bustling newsroom activity, to the shop floor worker on the shop floor, and so on. Relevance should always be the aim where possible [p. 112].

However, there is also a price one might have to pay for the "on-location" interview, especially of the "eyewitness" type. The background of the live interview, because it takes place during an on-going event, may be too distracting to what the interviewee is actually saying. Thus, for example, if an eyewitness is telling about a dramatic rescue and the camera enables the viewer to get even a glimpse of an injured person involved while the microphone might pick up the sound of an ambulance siren, all these stimuli would tend to mask the verbal message that the interviewee is trying to get across. Needless to say, all this "background information" is definitely relevant to the news *story,* but it might be considered as irrelevant to the actual interview. Considering the notion of control, which is our concern here, these kind of situations often "take over" and leave the reporter at a loss. As Yorke notes,

> There is a very fine line between a background of interest and one so absorbing that it distracts the viewer from what is being said [p. 112].

This may be considered to some degree as loss of control, which is part of the cost for such an interview.

Directness of the Broadcast

Another specific element relating to the notion of control, which is sometimes left to the reporter (or the news producer) is whether to do a "live" interview or to tape it for broadcast at a later time. This is, of course, part of the more general question of the use of live inserts in the newscast. The live segment creates a sense of immediacy, of "being there," and usually provides some heightened sense of drama. Not all stories can employ the live segment, however. Thus, for example, if the news item concerns a story that requires considerable investigative reporting and more than one interview, the interviews will obviously be taped, edited, and put together into one report. Also, if the newscast has very strict time constraints, as is the case with national networks in most countries, it will be difficult to conduct live interviews on the news.

Nevertheless, sometimes live interviewing does take place, particularly with highly experienced interviewers who know how to assert their control of the situation, and with the support of well-coordinated studio crews. And yet, the literature dealing with television news interviewing apparently does not seem to consider this point to be of sufficient significance to warrant any serious discussion of it.

Editing of Interviews

The final group of codes, that of editing the interviews, has already been alluded to. Let us now develop this point a bit further. Editing of recorded interviews entails two major aspects: substantive and technical. From the point of view of substance, editing enables the removal of part of an interview undesirable for one or more reasons. Thus editing can be used to simply shorten a longer interview, to remove an embarrassing situation on the part of the interviewer or interviewee, and to splice up the interview into several segments (for broadcast on different occasions) or in order to add visual segments or interview segments with other interviewees.

From the technical viewpoint, editing is used to insert an establishing shot of the interview setting, to add the wording of the questions not necessarily reported during the actual interview, to delete faulty recorded segments such as interference of outside background noises or changes in lighting conditions, to provide reaction shots of the interviewer, and to connect segments recorded on different reels of film or videotape.

Interestingly, not all of the texts that were examined here even mention the role of editing. This is perhaps reflected in what Siller (1972) describes as the ideal condition for a recorded interview:

> A 45-second take that is so entirely responsive to the situation that it simply can be lifted from the original and run on the air or included in a film or tape package [p. 149].

Gelles takes the same general position but expands on the time frame. As for the substantive aspect of the editing, he states,

> The perfect interview is one where an entire two or three minute section of film can be run unedited. Thus the reporter asks a couple of questions, gets satisfactory answers, and the entire uncut interaction is spliced into the evening film package [p. 33].

This is not often achieved, however, as will be demonstrated later. Moreover, according to Siller:

> The primary goal of editing filmed and video tape interviews is to wind up with a product in which edits cannot be detected by the home viewer (p. 147).

Whether or not this is true will be examined later. In any event, most of the discussion in the various texts, in the section on editing, is concerned with the technical aspects of how to do the "jump cut" or the "cut-away" shots, and how to prepare the reverse angle questions (see, for example, Fang, 1972: 109-111; and Tyrrell, 1972: 106-107).

It should also be noted that the editing of the interview is probably the greatest source of controversy among journalists and politicians and other public officials. As Yorke (1978) points out, prospective inter-viewees in countries where editorial freedom exists are aware of this dilemma and by submitting themselves to the interview, they accept the rules that govern the situation. Yorke's conclusion and recommen-dation is as follows:

> In all cases reporters should make it clear that they are under no obligation to use the whole of an interview, or indeed any of it, and give the subject an opportunity to make out a case in a cogent fashion or withdraw altogether [p. 110].

This seems to take us back to the notion of control, which closes the circle of the situational factors.

VERBAL CODES

There are two major verbal codes involving the formulation of the questions put to the interviewee and the rules of etiquette during the entire interview. Both are cited frequently in the literature.

Questioning Techniques

Formulating the questions for an interview is probably the most tricky and problematic area of the interview. Much has been written in the general literature on interviewing on how slight wording differences can lead to very different meanings. Moreover, when questions are asked orally, voice intonation can be a significant factor in connoting special shades of meaning and implications. All this clearly holds true for the television news interview. The wording of the questions is important not only for the interviewee but also for the audience. Since the interview is to be presented as part of a news item, the questions must be worded in such a way so that the viewer who is not all too familiar with the topic would be able to follow what is being discussed.

Several authors have noted the need for the interviewers to do their "homework." They recommend that the interviewer for television news read numerous newspapers and obtain background information on the topic as well as on the prospective interviewee. Some also talk about the need to get personally acquainted with the interviewee prior to conducting the interview.

Probably the first hard and fast rule is that the questions be short. As Dary (1971) put it bluntly: "They should be short and to the point" (p. 78). Moreover, the interviewer must formulate the questions so that they are relevant and meaningful or, as Fang (1972) puts it, "He should not embarrass his station, the man he interviews or himself by asking stupid questions" (p. 90).

Lewis (1984) also suggests that questions should be asked one at a time, without the use of compound questions. The latter, she argues, are more difficult to follow and to edit later on. Tyrrell (1972) argues that questions which can only lead to a "yes" or "no" answer should be avoided.

Most of the authors stress the importance of bringing to the interview a ready-made list of questions, either in actual written form or at least that the interviewer should have in his or her mind a clear notion of the questions that will be asked. The interview situation is a highly demanding one, and if the interviewer has to spend time thinking about what to ask, while listening to the responses of the interviewee, he or she might not manage the situation as effectively as would be desirable. Indeed, listening to the interviewee while he or she is speaking is a point all the authors agree on.

Some of the writers also suggest that the interviewer disclose to the interviewee the general nature of the questions prior to the interview, although none of the texts suggest that the exact wording of the questions be given ahead of time. As Yorke (1978) puts it:

> No journalist worth his salt ever compromises himself or his employees by submitting questions in advance [p. 116].

This practice may help put the interviewees at ease, especially if they are inexperienced in being interviewed. However, "practice" with the interviewee should be completely avoided because the second time a person answers a question is not as spontaneous as the first. After all, the interviewing situation is not designed to be a well-rehearsed performance (although many politicians and public officials indeed seem to like to use the interview as a stage on which they have the opportunity to play the leading or star role).

In addition to careful planning of the interview, the ability of the interview to be flexible and unpredictable is also considered to be a virtue. As Biagi (1986) puts it:

> A good interviewer always tries to carry the conversation forward to new ideas, new comments. The best questions are unexpected, the best answers are spontaneous. Predictable questions elicit predictable answers and lead to a predictable story. If you are constantly recapping or reviewing old material, or if you straitjacket yourself to a list of prepared questions, your interview will seem disorganized and disjointed [p. 82].

Rules of Etiquette

Much of the attention of the authors of the various texts has focused on what may be characterized as "rules of etiquette" of the interview, namely, how the participants should behave vis-a-vis toward one another, with the main emphasis on the interviewer's "treatment" of the interviewee. It seems, also, that if any aspect of the television news interview has been described somewhat differently by authors within the United States and Britain, and between the two countries, at least in the earlier years of television news, it is the way the interviewee should be treated.

Thus, for example, Green (1969), in the United States, says:

> Interviewing is in many cases a form of verbal fencing in which the reporter plans his attack in the hope of eliciting information which the interviewee may not wish to give. . . . It is the reporter's duty to ask questions which force the interviewee to defend his point of view, not questions which merely give him an opportunity to make a speech of his own choosing [p. 176].

On the other hand, Robin Day, a well-known British television interviewer, is quoted in Yorke (1978) as saying,

> A television interviewer is not employed as a debater, prosecutor, inquisitor, psychiatrist or third-degree expert, but as a journalist seeking information on behalf of the viewer [p. 115].

This basic attitude has also been expressed in the United States, however. Siller (1972), for example, states, "There is little to be gained for the reporter to approach an interview subject with the air of the grand inquisitor" (p. 143).

The "compromise" between these positions is expressed in the words of Lewis (1984) when she suggests: Approach the news source without being either subservient or aggressive (p. 123) or as Fang (1972) aptly titled one of the section in his book: "Toughness, sympathy, awareness, gall" (p. 96). Thus, the general attitude seems to stress firmness, on the one hand, and politeness, on the other hand.

NONVERBAL CODES

There are also nonverbal codes: those having to do with space, artifacts and the use of various filmic precedures. These, too, have been treated by those who have written about interviewing.

Spatial Codes

Interviewing for television news takes place in various kinds of settings. The literature has little to say about the spatial codes, however. There is one exception that relates to the spatial arrangement, namely, the use of eye contact. Several authors suggest that the interviewer maintain eye contact with the interviewee during the course of the interview. This is possible, of course, in face-to-face interviewing situations; but when the interview is conducted via an electronic hook-up and the interviewee is located in another place, such as in another studio, or on location, the eye contact notion becomes irrelevant.

As far as the distance between the reporter and the interviewee, it has been noted that several possibilities exist. And yet the literature does not seem to make any reference to this variable.

Artifactual Codes

The microphone is the main artifact used in the course of the interview. Some of the authors refer to this point. The general consensus is that the microphone be used as inconspicuously as possible. And yet, there does not seem to be perfect consensus about what kind of microphone to use. Thus, for example, Green (1969) says that:

> The hand-held mike is the worst offender because it calls attention to itself by its movement [p. 168]

whereas Shook (1982) says that:

> Microphones, another intimidating fact of television life, always should be held by the reporter and made as inconspicuous as possible [p. 69].

This, despite the fact that Shook does consider the miniature microphone pinned to the speaker's lapel as a possible solution.

Filmic Codes

The two filmic codes—the angle of the shooting of the interview and the degree of the closeness of the shot—get modest discussion in the literature. There is general consensus among the various authors that the more important aspect in the television news interview, as in any interview, is what is said by the interviewee and thus what is heard by the viewer, rather than what the interviewee looks like and how he or she is seen by the viewer. As Lewis (1984) succinctly put it: "Visuals are nice, but they remain secondary to substance" (p. 121). And yet, given the fact that the major distinction between the television news interview and any other journalistic interview is the fact that there is also a visual information channel, some discussion is given to this topic.

When an "establishing shot" is used in the interview, it is generally the first shot seen. It is the shot which gives the visual frame of reference for the interview. Thus, for example, the two participants in the interview are often shown sitting or standing together in some location (or sometimes walking together) which gives the viewer an indication of where and under what circumstances the interview is taking place. Sometimes the establishing shot is simply a few seconds of film or tape showing the interviewee with a voice over of the interviewer. The establishing shot is not used, however, in all television news interviews, especially when the interview segment is very brief, such as in the form of a "sound bite." This is probably the reason why the establishing shot is not discussed in most of the literature, with the exception of Siller (1972).

The actual filming of the interviewee is discussed in one way or another in most of the sources. Thus, given the consensus that the interviewee should be the focus of the interview, Tyrrell (1972), for example, notes that:

> Usually, the best angle is a three-quarter medium shot, followed by a head and shoulders close up and perhaps a bit close up [p. 106].

This quotation by Tyrrell actually sums up the three most common shots of the interviewee relating to the size of the image on the screen. The medium shot shows the interviewee at what may be considered a "social" distance, where the viewer can see some portion of the background, the interviewee's clothing, as well as the microphone being used (either the Lavalier or the hand held microphone). It is not far enough removed to give a better perspective of the general setting, the room, the furniture, as well as the table microphone, if such a microphone is being used. In the head and shoulders close up the viewer's television screen is filled with the image of the interviewee's face with some vague and generally out of focus background. This may be considered as the "personal" distance. The "big" close up (or what is sometimes termed a "tight" shot or an "extreme" close up shot), that is, the shot in which the camera zooms in to create an image from the chin to the forehead, allowing the viewer to see nothing but the whole or even only part of the interviewee's face. This may be considered as an "intimate" distance. As I indicated earlier, this kind of shot is "abnormal" in the sense that two people, even in the most intimate situation, cannot actually see each other at such a close distance and still maintain the image in focus. Whether or not this is considered as appropriate will be discussed later.

A slightly different terminology is used by Yorke (1978) in describing the various shots in the interview, accompanied by several graphic illustrations. When speaking of the work of the cameraman he says:

> He holds the first few questions and answers in a steady medium shot, from the waist up as the third question is being asked he tightens to a medium close-up, from the chest upwards; during the fifth he focuses in still further to a close-up of the head and shoulders [p. 120].

Two points are worth mentioning here. First, Yorke describes this sequence of shooting the interview as if it were a standard procedure, in which the cameraperson follows the same rules in every interview. And second, he fails to mention the extreme close-up shot from the chin to the forehead.

The literature on interviewing also discusses the "reaction shot" in which the reporter is seen, usually quite briefly, while the interviewee is answering a question. However, Siller (1972) objects to this term calling the "reaction shot" a misnomer. He argues that:

> Newsmen are not supposed to react to the remarks of an interview subject of anyone else in any way that could be taken to connote either approval of or disagreement with what the speaker is saying. It is permissible for the reporter to nod slightly to indicate understanding. To do more than that, facially or verbally, might be construed as editorial or something it should not be [p. 150].

Indeed, the "reaction" shot for the explicit purpose of providing a genuine reaction of the reporter is rarely shown, mainly due to the fact that most often only one camera is used, especially in on-location interviews. However, the "cutaway" shot, which sometimes resembles a "reaction" shot, is often used. In this kind of shot a brief insert of the reporter (or sometimes of a cameraperson) is shown, the purpose of which is to enable two segments of the interviewee's response to be edited together in a smooth transition while avoiding the "jump" shot. Otherwise, even an untrained viewer could notice that an edit was done.

CONCLUSION

In this chapter there is a brief discussion of what selected literature on television news interviewing says about some of the variables of interest.

I have not attempted to provide a complete review of the literature, but rather to highlight some of the points which I believe are central to understanding some of the approaches and techniques which are evident in television news interviewing.

In order to present this brief literature review I resorted to the four sets of codes of the interview: identity codes, verbal codes, nonverbal codes, and situational codes. In doing so, however, I did not give equal prominence to each set of codes and to their subdivisions, mainly because of the unequal treatment that each has received in the literature. In this sense, I have tried to present a fair reflection of the general way in which the literature has covered these various points.

In titling this chapter "Manual of Manuals" I do not mean to suggest that every item in the literature that I uncovered, part of which I presented here, presents the various points as mandatory for the reporter-interviewer, although it is often implied by the various authors that things should ideally be done in the manner suggested. Clearly, the task of the television news interviewer varies from interviewee to interviewee, and the personal style of interviewer as well as the techniques he or she uses are not the same (see, for example, Dennis and Rivers, 1974; and Dennis and Ismach, 1981). Thus we should definitely expect to find numerous departures and deviations from what has been recommended.

4

TV NEWS INTERVIEWING AT THE U.S. COMMERCIAL NETWORKS

A content analysis of all 514 interviews conducted during twelve evening newscasts on ABC, CBS, and NBC revealed that the interviews are very short, and that most deal with politics, internal order, human interest stories, and health and welfare. Most interviews take place in offices and public places, and are with males, serving as public officials. Some differences were found among the three networks.

The evening newscasts of the major commercial networks in the United States—ABC, CBS, and NBC—have a combined audience of millions and constitute the principal source of news for most Americans, according to the annual Roper poll. It is an assertion that goes undisputed in the United States, although the question of what people get out of the news is a different one which has been investigated and recently summarized by Robinson and Levy (1986).

Naturally, these highly visible news programs are also a major showcase for news interviews, a tool that is used both to deliver information and to make the news brisker and more vivid. Interviews break up the "talking heads" presentation of the news anchors as they go to the field for direct comments from what Nelson Algren called "people who know what they are talking about."

In spite of the extraordinary visibility of network news interviewing and its probable influence on local television interviewers who emulate national reporters and anchors "on their way to the top," an examination of the nature of network TV interviews is especially illuminating. Ironically, no previous systematic study of network television interviews exists, so this book presents new data about heretofore unexplored territory.

As indicated at the beginning of this book, I consider the comparative approach very useful in gaining a wider perspective of what things are like in a given setting or country. In other words, by comparing what things are like in different networks or in different countries it is possible to gain better insight and understanding of the topic under investigation. Thus one subject of comparative research in the field of television could be to examine how different stations or networks within a given country present the news. Another level of analysis could be to compare the news among different countries.

In this book both levels of analysis are presented. First, in this chapter, I shall discuss how interviews are conducted in network news in the United States, and I will present findings concerning the major evening newscasts of the three commercial networks: ABC's *World News Tonight,* CBS's *Evening News,* and NBC's *Nightly News.* In the next chapter, I shall present the findings of a similar analysis conducted in three additional countries: Britain, West Germany, and Israel.

The choice of these four countries was partly on theoretical grounds and also somewhat a result of convenience. In the course of another research project which has to do with the presentation and perception of social conflicts in television news, several colleagues and I recorded the evening news in several countries. Those recordings served as the raw material for the social conflicts study as well as for this study of television news interviewing.

As for the United States, Britain, West Germany, and Israel, all these countries represent Western democracies, in which the press is based on essentially the same social principles and values as well as on similar journalistic norms and techniques. At the same time, however, the media organizations in these countries are quite different, ranging from the highly commercialized system in the United States to the totally noncommercial organization in Israel (with Britain and West Germany somewhere in between). Also, and related to this, is the extent to which the respective governments exercise control, supervise, or merely attempt to influence the broadcasting system.

As indicated, the variables that I selected for examination are based on the theoretical concepts and notions that I have presented earlier, as well as on countless hours that I have devoted to watching television news interviews. Thus some of the variables are more closely tied to the taxonomies that were presented in the first two chapters, and others are based primarily on heuristic and subjective conclusions derived from my own viewing. I have also constructed some additional variables that are derivations of those explicated above.

One final comment: Upon first encountering the above list of variables, the American reader, who is highly familiar with the way interviewing is done on television news in the United States, may wonder why some of them were included in the analysis. After all, he or she may think, the phenomena revealed by some of the variables hardly, if ever, exist in the newscasts of the U.S. networks. This may indeed be true, as the findings of the analysis will shortly indicate. However, this is precisely why the comparative research paradigm has been adopted here. That is, if something does not occur in the *United States* it doesn't necessarily mean that it simply doesn't exist at all. Only comparative research can illustrate this in no uncertain terms.

SAMPLING OF NEWSCASTS

The decision concerning what sample to use was taken by the research team of the social conflict study. The major evening newscasts were videotaped on the following 12 days in 1984: January 16-19, 23-26, 30-31, and February 1-2. These days consisted of all Mondays through Thursdays during a consecutive three-week period. Weekend newscasts were not used since they are somewhat different from weekday newscasts in some of the countries. Thus by selecting only weekdays, we kept tighter control over the kinds of content and the formats of the newscasts. Thus we have a total of 36 U.S. newscasts, 12 for each of the three networks. Also, we have 12 newscasts for each of the following broadcasting systems: BBC in Britain, ARD and ZDF in West Germany, and IBA in Israel. The interviews were coded by pairs of graduate students who have good command of the language of the interviews as well as familiarity with the newscasts of the relevant countries.

Basically, the sample is sufficiently large to warrant generalizations to other points in time. However, as is always the case when drawing a sample, there is sampling error. This means that there is the possibility that some unusual occurrence might have skewed the results in one way or another. This problem of specificity is particularly evident in research on news since no two newscasts are ever exactly alike just as no two days ever produce the same events and stories. However, since it is virtually impossible to know how unique or extraordinary one's sample is, the best one can do is to attempt to explain what seem to be possible departures using whatever additional information is available. The reader should keep this in mind when considering the findings.

GENERAL CHARACTERISTICS OF THE
U.S. NEWS INTERVIEWS

For the present analysis I was interested only in news items that contained interviewing. Accordingly, each news item that contained at least one interview was examined and coded.

Interviewing Parameters
in the Three Networks

Before examining the specific variables, let us present some general information concerning the scope of interviewing on the three U.S. networks. As indicated, the findings concerning the U.S. networks are based on 12 newscasts per network, or a total of 36 newscasts. Of the 612 news items, 191 (or 31%) contained at least one interview, there was a total of 514 interviews, including a grand total of 657 interview clips (a clip was defined as a segment of an interview containing one or more question or response; a news item could contain more than one clip of the same interview if the different segments are separated by visual information, an interview with another person, or the reporter's text). Table 1 presents the most salient statistical information.

The findings in Table 1 indicate that the three networks do not differ in any meaningful way in terms of the number of news items each contains. NBC had 195 items, or 16.25 items per newscast; ABC had 208 items, or 17.33 items per newscast; and CBS with its 209 items had essentially the same as ABC. Thus with respect to the number of items, the three networks have essentially the same structure. Moreover, as is well known, the length of the newscasts of the three networks is the same, thus the average length of each item is virtually the same.

Also, as Table 1 indicates, the greatest number of news items containing at least one interview was found in the NBC newscasts (68 items), CBS follows suit with 67 items, and ABC has the fewest number of items with interviews (56 items). In other words, 27% of ABC's news items contained interviews; in CBS, 32% of the items contained at least one interview; and NBC with 35% had relatively the highest figure. Thus the general use of interviews in the three networks was about the same.

TABLE 1
General Statistics on Television News Interviewing in U.S. Networks

	ABC	CBS	NBC
Number of news items	208	209	195
Overall number of interviews	117	214	183
Overall number of interview clips	143	285	229
Percentage of news items with at least one interview	27	32	35
Average number of interviews per story	2.1	3.2	2.7
Average length of interview (in seconds)	16.2	12.8	12.2
Range of interview length (in seconds)	1-120	1-75	1-142
Percentage of time devoted to interviews in newscast	12	17	14

However, as for the actual number of interviews in the newscasts, Table 1 shows that there were significant differences among the three networks. CBS presented a total of 214 interviews in the 12 newscasts studied, NBC followed relatively close behind with 183 interviews, but ABC had only 117 interviews. Thus the average number of interviews per newscast is 17.8 for CBS; 15.3 for NBC; and only 9.8 for ABC. Another way of looking at these figures indicates that the mean number of interviews in news item containing at least one interview puts CBS on top once again with 3.2 interviews per news item; NBC follows suit with 2.7 interviews per item; and ABC still ranks lowest with 2.1 interviews per item.

Most interviews within a news item consisted of only one clip. The situation with regard to the three networks was as follows: At ABC, of the 117 interviews, 86% had only one clip; at CBS, only 72% of the 214 interviews consisted of one clip; and at NBC 79% of the 183 interviews had one clip. The average number of clips per interview was 1.22 for ABC, 1.25 for NBC, and 1.33 for CBS.

The next characteristic on the agenda is the average duration of an interview as well as the proportion of the entire newscast that is devoted to interviewing. This information appears in the bottom part of Table 1. Accordingly, during the time period reviewed by our sample, the overall figures indicate that CBS's *Evening News* used more interviews than the other two networks, and ABC's *World News Tonight* had the least amount of interviewing. At the same time, ABC's interviews were, on average, the longest in duration.

This point concerning the length of the interviews needs some elaboration since the range of the duration of the interviews (or "sound bites"), from 1 to 142 seconds, does not give the whole picture. Of the 514 American interviews, 3 were one-second long, 18 were two-seconds long, 23 were three-seconds long, 35 were four-seconds long, and 41 were five-seconds long. In other words, 110 of the 514 interview (or 21%) were five seconds or less in duration. Here are three examples, one for each network.

ABC World News Tonight did a story on January 26, 1984, on Louisiana's then governor-elect Edwin Edwards's campaign that took him all the way to Paris, France. Among the people interviewed were some U.S. tourists in Paris. One woman (unidentified) said, "We're having fun in Paris" (two seconds) and the mayor of Paris, Jacques Chirac (today's French prime minister) is interviewed and all we hear him say is: "Superb, superb!" (two seconds).

On the same day on *NBC Nightly News,* Bill Schechner is doing a story on a young girl who has a dream of winning an Olympic medal.

Here is a brief segment from the story:

> Schechner: One thousand miles away near Chicago, Edie's family. Her parents have negotiated a new mortgage on their home to pay for her training; and they set a strict time table for her progress.
>
> Father: She's on a track (one second).
>
> Mother: On a track (one second).
>
> Schechner: How do you know?
>
> Mother: Because . . .

The *CBS Evening News* example is from January 31st, in which Bob Schieffer does a piece on a sculptor in New Hampshire who carved the images of some of the presidential candidates out of ice. At one point the text is as follows:

> Schieffer: People here are used to politicians at this time of year, but with the campaign heating up, front-runner Mondale is having problems too.
>
> Woman (unidentified): They've been around here enough, so you can't help but recognize them.
>
> Man (also unidentified): Did a nice job (one second).
>
> Woman: Yeah, I think . . .

In sum, each of the networks presents very brief interviews as standard practice, and yet the three networks presented overall different amounts of interviews in their respective newscasts.[1]

THE VARIABLES EXAMINED

Now that we have looked at the overall prevalence of news interviews, let us turn to the detailed examination of some of the substantive characteristics of the interviews. The complete list of variables that we turn to composes the majority of the interview codes under the general headings of identity codes, situational codes, verbal codes, and non-verbal codes. Some of the specific codes do not appear in the present chapter, however, since they were not empirically examined. Moreover, in the presentation of the findings I make two additional distinctions: First, I distinguish, when it is relevant, between characteristics of the interviewer and the interviewee; and second, for some of the variables, I report both on the frequency of occurrence as well as on the duration (as I have just done for the overall characteristics of the interviews). The reader may wish, at any time, to refer back to Chapter 2, where the classification of the codes is initially presented and explicated.

IDENTITY VARIABLES

The first group of variables on which I wish to compare the three U.S. networks is based on the notion of the identity codes. These variables are not specific identity codes of the interviewer or the interviewee, however; rather, they refer to the "identity" of the interview as a whole. Three such variables are examined here: the general topic of the news item containing the interview; the prominence of interviews in social conflict items; and the language of the interview.

Topics of Interview Items

The major variable examined that relates to the news item as a whole is the general *topic* of the item. Based on the newscasts, 14 topic categories were defined: internal politics, international politics, defense, internal order (for example, demonstrations, civil war, and so on), economics, labor, business, transportation, agriculture, health and welfare, population and immigration, education, press and communication, housing, environment, energy, science and technology, social relations, disasters and accidents, sports, culture, ceremonial, human interest, and a remaining category for "other" undefined topics. Despite the difficulty encountered in assigning some of the items to general categories of this kind (which occurs in most content-analytic studies of news) it seems that this list is sufficiently exhaustive and that the categories are by and large mutually exclusive of one another. This classification tells us in what kind of stories interviews are used, and in what kind of stories they are not. The occurrence of interviews in the various topics in the three networks is presented in Table 2.

The most striking general finding is the difference in the patterns of the distributions of the interview topics in the three networks. Thus the rankings for none of the pairs of networks are the same. Note, for example, the wide gaps between the networks with regard to stories on internal order, human interest, health and welfare, disasters and accidents, defense, and sports. These findings are even more interesting in view of the overall general similarity in the distribution of the actual topics of *news items* in the three U.S. networks, as has been studied and documented by several researchers. Moreover, what is even more meaningful is to compare the distribution of the topics in which interviews were conducted with the general distribution of the topics in the newscasts of the three networks on the same twelve days. This

TABLE 2
News Interviews by Topic Categories and Network (in percentages)

Topics	ABC (117)	CBS (214)	NBC (183)	Total (514)
Internal politics	24	16	19	19
Internal order	9	8	20	12
Human interest	6	10	17	11
Health and welfare	9	15	5	10
International politics	9	8	4	7
Economics	7	8	4	6
Business	5	4	8	6
Disasters and accidents	1	8	3	5
Defense	–	8	2	4
Sports	8	2	4	4
Education	7	2	2	3
Science and technology	2	5	2	3
Social relations	3	3	2	3
Other	10	3	8	7

comparison would indicate whether or not the interviews are conducted according to the distribution of the topics among all the news items, or whether interviews are more likely to appear in certain topics more than in others.

For the sake of brevity, let us examine this for the three networks combined. It seems that in many of the topic categories the percentage of items *with* interviews is very close to the overall percentage of that topic among all the news items. Thus, for example, while 21% of all the news items were concerned with internal politics, 19% of all the interviews were on topics involving internal politics; also, 12% of the news items involved internal order, and the same percentage of all the interviews were in that category; a similar picture was obtained for economic items, for items on disasters and accidents, and for items dealing with social relations.

However, some topic categories were overrepresented among the interviews. Thus, for example, whereas about 3% of all the items dealt with health and welfare, as many as 10% of all the interviews were in that topic category; also, only 7% of the items were categorized as human interest stories, whereas 11% of all the interviews were in that category. And conversely, some topic categories were underrepresented in the interviews: For example, 21% of all the news items dealt with international politics, whereas only 7% of the interviews were in that category; and finally, 13% of all the items dealt with business with only 6% of all the interviews occurring in business items.

What this means is that interviews in television news are not conducted in all topic categories according to the overall relative frequency of the topics. It seems that topics involving *people* (for instance, human interest and health and welfare) have more interviews, whereas topics involving institutions and policy, such as politics among nations and business (including stock market reports and similar items) will have relatively fewer interviews.

Interviews in Social Conflict Items

Additional support for this argument is found if we examine the extent to which interviews are presented in items that do or do not depict social conflict. Since the news recordings come from a study on social conflict in television news, these data are also available. In that study, social conflicts were defined as "confrontation between groups or representatives of groups with relation to goals or means to obtain goals." Thus, for example, if man robs bank because man is hungry and in need of money, that kind of story would not be considered a social conflict; however, if man robs bank because he wishes to protest against the economic system of society, then that would be considered as a social conflict. Using this definition, of all the ABC interviews, 55% are in items containing social conflict; as for CBS, 49% of the interviews are in social conflict news stories; and at NBC the respective figure is 62%. Thus half or more of the interviews are presented in stories that contain social conflict, with some variability indicated among the three networks.

To be meaningful, these data should be compared with the overall level of social conflicts reported in the newscasts. Accordingly, in the ABC newscasts, 45% of the news items contained social conflict; at CBS 54% contained social conflict; and at NBC 49% of these items contained social conflict. Thus the finding concerning the level of conflict in items with interviews generally supports the notion that conflict items are more likely to have interviews, probably because the various parties to the conflict are given the opportunity to express their positions. This was clearly the case for ABC and for NBC, although not for CBS.

Language of the Interview

The question of the *language* of the interview, that is, whether or not it was in the native language of the country of broadcast and whether or not *translation* was offered (if the interview was not in the native tongue) was also examined. This was done because it provided some indication of the extent to which the newscasts could be considered ethnocentric.

Newscasts solely in the language of the country of broadcast (for instance, English in the case of the United States), even if they contain items from foreign lands, could be characterized as more ethnocentric. The use of other languages, despite the worldwide dominance of the English language, could be indicative, to some extent, of this cultural issue.

In the United States the use of non-English speaking interviews is very infrequent. Of the 514 interviews on the three U.S. networks, only 7 (or 1.4%) were with interviewees who spoke a language other than English. Of all the ABC interviews analyzed, 97% were conducted in English; in the CBS newscasts 99% of the interviews were done in English; and at NBC there was not a single case of an interview being conducted in a language other than English.

Moreover, in the few cases where translation was provided for what the non-English speaking interviewee was saying, it was always done by means of an English voice-over by a person of the same gender as the interviewee. Thus although the numbers are extremely small, it is interesting to note that of these five cases, only one interview was not translated at all and was left in the original (Spanish) language.

Gender and Role of Interviewers

The next set of variables examined are *specific* identity variables, that is, having to do with the identity of the interviewer and the interviewee, and not the general characteristics of the interview itself. First, we were interested in *who* the interviewer was. Thus we coded the *gender* of the interviewer and his or her *role* in the newscast (that is, whether the interviewer was a reporter or an anchorperson).

The person conducting the interview in the newscast can have several roles: that of the anchorperson, the correspondent who presents the story, or another reporter who provided the interview for the news item (as a matter of fact, many of the interviews conducted for news stories are not conducted by the reporters who present the stories but by "field producers," "researchers," or reporters from a network affiliate that are later spliced into the packages that the more visible correspondents appear in). All available cues were used to determine who was doing the interview, such as the visual presence or merely the voice of the interviewer. In all three U.S. networks, the news anchors conducted only 24 of the 514 interviews (4.7%). This was most pronounced at NBC where the anchor (Tom Brokaw) conducted 14 interviews (in some cases the interviewee was another network person). At ABC the anchor (Peter Jennings) conducted a total of six interviews, and at CBS the anchor (Dan Rather) conducted only four interviews.

As for the nonanchor interviewers, it seems that in numerous cases, due to the filming and editing techniques used, the interviewer is neither seen nor heard. Since the criterion for determining the gender of the interviewer was based on actually hearing or seeing him or her, in numerous interviews making such an affirmative determination was not possible. Thus at ABC the identity of the interviewer was not certain in 47% of the interviews, at CBS in 53% of the interviews, and at NBC in 77% of the interviews. It should be noted that these figures are either equal to (in the case of NBC) or lower than the figures for the identity of the interviewer since the gender of the anchorperson was always known (and is male). Female interviewers were positively identified in only 22 cases: 7 at ABC, 5 at CBS, and 10 at NBC (6%, 2%, and 5% respectively).

Role Characteristics of the Interviewees

In order to obtain a profile of the identity of the interviewees, several variables pertaining to the nature and roles of the interviewee were coded. Some of these variables are inherent to the interviewee while others are only meaningful within the particular context of the interview. Thus in the general context, we looked at the *gender of the interviewee* and whether or not he or she was a *native* (or at least a resident) person in the country in which the interview was broadcast. Also, we checked to see if the interviewee was a *public official*, whether or not he or she was a *professional* or *expert* person. As for the specific context of the interview, we checked whether or not the person was chosen at *random*, and whether he or she was a *victim* or *involved* in the story being reported. Finally, it was determined if *captions* were used to indicate the identity of the interviewee.

Table 3 presents these findings. (It should be noted that the percentages of the identity variables can exceed 100%, as each person can be characterized by more than one trait—for instance, a person can be a public official as well as an expert).

As the table illustrates, the great majority of the interviewees in the evening newscasts of the three U.S. networks are men, whereas women represent only 14%-18% of the samples, depending on the network. Also, only 3% to 6% of the interviewees are non-Americans.

As for the "status" or "role" variables, it seems that across the board the interviewees are *not* overwhelmingly public officials, experts, or persons elected to their positions. There are some differences among the three networks, with somewhat fewer public officials and professionals/experts in the NBC newscasts as compared with those of ABC and CBS.

TABLE 3
Summary of Identity Variables of the Interviewees
by Network (in percentages)

	ABC (117)	CBS (214)	NBC (183)
Gender of interviewee (male)	86	82	83
Native to country of broadcast	97	94	96
Public official	48	41	25
Elected to position	31	28	26
Professional/expert	44	52	29
Random selection	32	45	50
Victim	23	24	25
Involved	88	83	87

Finally, half or more of the interviewees on the news are *not* selected in a random fashion, a fact particularly marked in the ABC newscasts. This point is further reinforced when considering that 83% or more of the interviewees are directly involved in the stories in which they appear as interviewers. On the other hand, the frequency of appearance of "victims" is relatively low in all three networks, despite the fact that half or more of the stories in which interviewees appear are conflicts, the sort of item that quite often may involve victims of some act or situation.[2]

Explicit Identification of the Interviewees

The final identity variable of the interviewee that we looked at was the use of verbal and visual references (printed captions) used with regard to the identity of the interviewee during the interview. We found at CBS that in 52% of the interviews there was no reference made to the identity of the interviewee, neither verbally nor by means of a printed caption on the screen. At ABC in only 29% of the cases was there no reference and at NBC in 24% of the cases. NBC seemed to be highest in the use of only verbal references (in 23% of the interviews), whereas at ABC and CBS this occurred in 7% of the interviews. Only visual captions were used in ABC most often (58%) and in 39%-40% at the other two networks. Finally, NBC used both verbal and visual references in 13% of the cases, whereas this practice was used at ABC in 6% of the interviews and at CBS in only 2% of the cases.

Finally, the average length of time that visual captions appeared on the screen was 2.2 seconds at ABC, 1.9 seconds at CBS, and 1.5 seconds at NBC. The low figure for NBC, which is hardly enough time for the average person to read the caption, was probably compensated for by the fact that NBC used more verbal references than the other two networks.

SITUATIONAL VARIABLES

The second set of variables has to do with the situation or general context of the interview. Specifically, we looked at four main points: the *location* (studio or on location); the physical *background* of the interview (in an office, in a home, and so on); whether the interview was presented *live* or whether it was *prerecorded*; and whether or not the interview was *edited* or presented in its entirety.

The Location of the Interview

Of all the 514 interviews examined, clearly most (95.5%) took place at some out-of-studio location. At ABC 97% of the interviews were at an out-of-studio location, at CBS 96% were out-of-studio, and at NBC 94% of the interviews were conducted out of the studio.

Of the remaining 23 interviews in all the U.S. networks, 12 were conducted in one of three formats: in-the-studio with both the interviewer and interviewee present; studio-to-location where the interviewee (anchorperson) was in the studio and the interviewee at some other location; and studio-to-studio, in which case the interviewer (anchor) spoke to his interviewee, who was in a studio at a different location. In the final 11 cases it was impossible to determine the location due to the nature of the interview segment shown.

The Background of the Interview

The background of the interview refers to the specific physical setting in which the interview was conducted. Table 4 provides the distribution for the kinds of locations in which the interviews were conducted. A general place of work is defined as a factory, a store, a hospital, and so on, but not including an office. Interviews that were conducted in an office were coded separately. The "nature" category refers to settings in which the interviewer and interviewee were standing or sitting in an out-of-doors garden setting or the like. Interviews coded as being held in government buildings are those conducted in nonoffice settings (for instance, lobbies, at the doorway, outside a committee room, and so on). Interviews in the home setting were coded as such. Public places refer to locations such as street, beaches, sports facilities, and the like. If the exact location of the interview could not be coded, but it was clear that it was not in a studio, it was so stated and included in the final category of the table.

It should be noted that there was much similarity among the three networks as to the locations of the interviews. The only exceptions were with the interviews conducted in an out-of-doors setting (with relatively

TABLE 4
Locations of the Interviews by Network (in percentages)

	ABC (117)	CBS (214)	NBC (183)
General place of work	12	9	10
Clearly visible office	26	32	29
Nature (out-of-doors)	7	9	15
Government building	11	5	4
At home	7	8	6
Public place	21	26	25
Studio	2	2	2
Could not be determined	14	9	9

more such interviews at NBC) and with interviews in government buildings (with relatively more in ABC newscasts).

Live Versus Prerecorded and Edited Interviews

Nearly all the interviews shown in the newscasts of the three U.S. networks were prerecorded and edited. Overall, only 8 interviews (1.6%) were done "live"; at ABC 3 interviews (or 2.6%) were done live; at CBS 4 interviews (1.9%); and at NBC only one interview was done live (0.5%).

VERBAL VARIABLES

The verbal codes have to do with the questioning techniques and the rules of etiquette. Thus, generally speaking, the variables having to do with the verbal codes of the interview relate to the *interaction* during the interview. From the *interviewer's* point of view they deal with the *number of questions* put by the interviewer to the interviewee and heard in the newscast; the number of *repeated* questions; the number of *provocative* questions heard; and the number of *interruptions* of the interviewee by the interviewer. The verbal "presence" of the interviewer was determined by the amount of time the interviewer was *heard talking* during the interview (that is, asking questions). Finally, we examined whether or not the interviewer referred to the interviewee by his or her *first name.*

From the *interviewee's* point of view three variables were examined: whether or not the interviewee referred to the interviewer by his or her *first name;* whether or not "role switching" took place, that is, did the interviewee at any point in the interview assume the role of interviewer and begin to ask the interviewer questions; and finally, the verbal "presence" of the interviewee during the interview was determined by the amount of time the interviewee was heard talking, that is, answering questions.

Number of Questions Heard

The questions and the answers constitute the basic ingredients of an interview. And yet, in numerous television news interviews, as presented on the screen, no question is heard. It is assumed, of course, that the interviewee is asked a question, but in many cases, due to editing and "packaging" considerations, the question is omitted from the news item.

Thus in the U.S. newscasts examined, of the 191 items that contained interviews, in only 16 items (or 8% of the interviews) were any questions presented by the interviewer heard by the audience. Interestingly, however, when an interview did contain at least one question, it was quite likely to contain more. Thus at ABC a total of 24 questions were heard, at CBS 23 questions were heard, and at NBC a total of 27 questions were actually heard, for a total of 74 questions on all three networks.

Taking into account the 16 interviews only that had any audible questions, there was an average of 4.6 questions per interview. The overall average, however, indicates that given the great number of interviews without a single question heard, at ABC the viewer could hear an average of 0.21 questions per interview, at CBS one could hear only 0.11 questions per interview, and at NBC the respective figure was 0.15 questions per interview.

Repeated and Provocative Questions
and Interruptions

Two specific aspects of the questions that were actually heard were examined: the number of repeated questions and the number of provocative questions. A repeated question is one that is put to the interviewee either in the exact same words or in a paraphrased fashion, but highly similar to the original question. This questioning format is sometimes used when the interviewee does not reply adequately to the original question. In all the U.S. newscasts examined, only 3 of the 74 questions were coded as repeated questions.

A provocative question was one in which some rhetorical device was used, by wording and/or by voice intonation, either to make a point by the interviewer or to discredit the interviewee (for instance, a "rhetorical question"). This technique was used in the U.S. newscasts a total of 18 times, which represents 24% of all the questions heard. The situation differed, however, from network to network: At ABC only one question (4%) was provocative, at CBS seven questions (30%) of those heard were provocative, and at NBC ten questions (37%) of the questions heard were provocative.

Finally, the phenomenon in which the interviewer interrupted the interviewee was almost entirely absent. In all the U.S. newscasts in the sample, there were only four such cases seen on the screen.

Verbal "Presence" of the Interviewer

On the average, in each interview the interviewer was heard talking 1.2 seconds at ABC and 0.7 seconds at CBS and at NBC. Summing across the three networks, the total audio "presence" of the interviewers (that is, the total amount of time they were heard speaking) was 2%-3% of the total time of the interviews. (Note that at ABC and CBS the interviewer was seen for more time than he or she was heard, whereas in NBC this was slightly reversed. This is possible, however, as sometimes a question is asked by the interviewer while the face of the interviewee is actually seen on the screen.)

The Use of First Names
by the Interviewer

Part of the notion of the rules of etiquette of the interview is the way the interviewer approaches his or her interviewee. Specifically, one of the devices that can be used in certain situations is to refer to the interviewee by his or her first name. This is hardly ever done in the national network news in the United States, although the practice is more common in local news (see Chapter 7). Thus at ABC the interviewee was approached by the interviewer by his first name in 7% of the interviews, but this was mainly when Peter Jennings interviewed Pierre Salinger, who was in Paris, or when Jennings interviewed David Brinkley in two commentary segments in the studio (these segments were coded as interviews, as they were conducted in a question and answer format). At CBS, in only 1% of the interviews was a first name reference made, and at NBC this occurred in 2% of the interviews.

The Use of First Names
by the Interviewee

First names use on the part of the interviewee was also examined. As with the interviewers, there were virtually no cases of the interviewee calling the interviewer by his or her first name. The only exceptions to this were, as just noted above, when network people such as commentators, serving as interviewees, were asked questions by the anchors, in which case the commentator referred to the anchor by his first name.

Role Switching

As for role switching, that is, a situation in which the interviewee responded to a question or comment of the interviewer by asking a question, a total of only five such cases occurred, all of which were at CBS. Here are two examples:

On January 17th, 1984, Dan Rather reported on the arrest in London's Heathrow Airport of Linda McCartney, wife of Paul McCartney, on suspicion of possessing marijuana.

Rather: The 41-year-old former Beatle appeared unconcerned by the Barbados arrest, his fourth such run-in with the law. He was asked if, after all this, he still would smoke marijuana.

McCartney: Are you?

On January 24th Ike Pappas did an ironic story in New Hampshire on Ernest Hollings, at the time one of the Democratic contenders for the presidential nomination. Pappas interviews a woman in a restaurant. At one point the woman begins to "interview" Pappas.

Pappas: How about the name Hollings?

Woman: No, it really doesn't. Is he a presidential candidate?

Pappas: Yes, he is.

Hollings seen saying: And we need a president who can reach out and give us that sense of purpose.

Women: What is his party?

Pappas: What is his party? He's a Democrat.

Woman: He's a Democrat?

Pappas: Are you a Democrat?

Woman: Yes, I am.

Obviously at no time does the real interviewee become the interviewer, but the situation in which the reporter is asked questions, even if at times rhetorical questions, is interesting and noteworthy.

Verbal "Presence" of the Interviewee

Finally, the proportion of time the interviewee was heard talking during the course of the complete interview ranged from 86% on ABC to 92% on CBS, with NBC presenting the interviewee talking during 91% of the interview. The respective average amounts of time the interviewee was heard talking was: 12.6 seconds at ABC, 11.2 seconds at CBS, and 10.7 at NBC.

It should be noted that the combined amount of time that the interviewer is seen and heard can exceed the total amount of time of the interview as both are independent of one another and were counted accordingly. Also, the combined proportions of time that the interviewer and interviewee are heard speaking is not necessarily equal to 100%, since there are some segments in which neither of them is heard talking, such as during an establishing shot, usually at the beginning of the interview, when both the interviewer and the interviewee are seen with a voice-over by the correspondent.

NONVERBAL VARIABLES

The nonverbal variables that were examined are a reflection of the spatial codes, the artifactual codes, and the filmic codes: The spatial codes we looked at dealt with the physical arrangement of the interviewer vis-à-vis the interviewee; the use of microphones is an example of an artifactual code; and the kinds of shots used to frame the interviewees is the filmic code that was selected.

The Spatial-Physical Arrangement

Two related aspects of the spatial and physical arrangement of the interviews were examined: the distance between the interviewer and the interviewee and the posture of the interviewee. It should be noted that both these variables are determined on the basis of what can be seen on the screen, hence quite often it was impossible to make a clear determination due to the frame used (that is, usually because of the use of only a close-up shot it was not possible to see anything other than the face of the interviewee).

At ABC, in 12% of the interviews the distance between the interviewer and interviewee was small (up to 3 feet); in 12% it was medium (between 3 and 6 feet—usually behind a desk or similar piece of furniture); in 3% the distance was great—more than six feet; finally, in 73% of the cases it was impossible to tell how far the participants were from one another. Of all the ABC interviews, the interviewee was sitting in 49% of the interviews; standing in 41%; in motion (in a vehicle or walking) in 2%; and impossible to tell in 8% of the cases. At CBS, in 14% of the interviews the distance was small, in 42% it was medium; in 4% it was great; and in 40% it was impossible to tell. Also, in 47% of the cases the interviewee was sitting, in 38% he or she was standing, in 1% the interviewee was in motion, and in 14% of the cases it was impossible to tell. Finally, at NBC, in 38% of the interviews the distance was small, in 13% it was medium, there were no cases in which the interview participants were clearly far from one another, and in 49% it was impossible to tell. As for the posture, in 44% of the cases the interviewee was sitting, in 48% he or she was standing, in 1% he or she was in a reclining position, and in 7% it was impossible to tell.

The Kind of Microphones Used

As for the microphone, several possibilities exist: the lavalier, the hand mike, the table mike, and the shotgun mike (held by a soundperson below the picture frame). The choice of which will be used in a given interview is sometimes determined by the interview setting and some-times seems to be based on the preference of the reporter. However, when examining the news product, namely, the newscast as it appears on the screen, it is quite often difficult, if not impossible, to determine the kind of microphone used. Table 5 presents the different microphones used in the U.S. interviews.

Due to the filming and editing techniques used at the three networks, it seems that at ABC it was generally easier for the coders to determine the kind of microphone being used, whereas at CBS it was most difficult. Moreover, at ABC we found more use of hand-held microphones than in other networks. It is possible, however, that the other networks also use more hand-held microphones but due to the framing of the pictures the microphone could not be seen on the screen.

Visual Presence and the
Framing of the Interviewee

As noted earlier, the interviewee should be, and in fact is, the main focal point of the interview. In the ABC newscasts the interviewee was seen for an average of 14.8 seconds per interview, at CBS he or she was seen for an average duration of 11.9 seconds, and in the NBC interviews the interviewee was seen for an average of 11.5 seconds. For all three networks, this represents 94%-96% of the entire interviews.

As for the various shots used (medium shot, close-up shot, and extreme close-up shot), there are some differences among the networks.

TABLE 5
Use of Microphones by Network (in percentages)

	ABC (117)	CBS (214)	NBC (183)
Lavalier	9	5	11
Hand held	13	4	7
Soundman, table mike	2	–	–
Cannot determine	76	91	82

TABLE 6
Time Interviewee Seen by Type of Shot and Network (in percentages)

	ABC (117)	CBS (214)	NBC (183)
Medium shot	41	17	21
Close-up shot	51	72	65
Extreme close-up shot	2	5	5
Cannot determine	6	6	9

Table 6 presents the proportion of time that each of the three shots was used by the three networks. The "medium" shot was defined as a frame from the chest upward, the "close-up" was defined as a frame from the neck upward, and the "extreme close-up" shot was defined as a frame from the chin to the forehead.

The findings in Table 6 indicate that the visual frame most prevalent in all three networks was the close-up. However, in CBS the use of this shot was highly dominant (72%) as compared to only 51% at ABC. On the other hand, ABC used the medium shot relatively more than any other network and used the extreme close-up shot only on rare occasions.

CONCLUSION

The findings presented in this chapter present a difficult dilemma. Since we are involved in a two-level comparative project, first among the U.S. networks and then among the four countries, the question is how different must the findings among the three networks be in order for us to conclude that the differences are meaningful. It is not the intention here to get into the statistical meaning of the term "significant" difference.[3] Rather, we need to have some substantive yardstick that will be useful to draw such conclusions. It seems that the best way to approach this issue is to have some rationale whereby we can explain the differences we obtained, otherwise we might opt to suggest that the differences are due to sampling error, mainly the result of the fact that no two newscasts are ever alike in terms of the selection of new items as well as in terms of their composition, that is, how they are put together.

Given the obtained differences that may be valid and not due to chance, it must be admitted that there is no simple explanation for them. It would be nice if we could develop a theoretical rationale (or to find one in the literature) that will explain the differences among the networks. This approach is not likely to succeed, however. As I indicated earlier, is it not entirely clear why we should expect to find differences among ABC, CBS, and NBC on various points concerning the way interviews are used in the news. Is there something about the three news organizations that will cause them to operate differently in this regard? Indeed, numerous studies have been conducted on various aspects of television news in the United States and very few meaningful and consistent differences have been found.

Another approach might be to talk with some of the people concerned with the production and presentation of interviews in television news and to try to learn from them how they might explain some of the differences. This would be especially useful if it were felt that some differences may be due to the personal styles of the people who do the news interviews, rather than being based on some grand theory. In fact, what I have done is to speak to a number of persons in all four countries who are closely familiar with the way television news interviewing is done in their respective networks. I shall delay presenting what they had to say, however, until the cross cultural findings are analyzed. Let us, therefore, turn now to look at the way interviews are done in the news in Britain, West Germany, and Israel.

NOTES

1. I wish to pause for a moment and discuss the critical question of the extent to which the sample with which I have been working is representative of the U.S. network newscasts in general. I have raised this issue before when I described the sample used, and I would like to elaborate on this a bit given these initial findings on the differences between the three networks. Clearly two possibilities exist: Either the sample in this study is indeed biased, which will be difficult if not impossible to disprove without some convincing evidence; or the three networks actually differ in their use of interviewing. Naturally the latter possibility is more desirable, thereby rejecting the possibility that the sample is biased. Fortunately, there seems to be some recent evidence that clearly lends support to this interpretation.

This evidence comes from a recently completed doctoral dissertation by Schneider (1985) entitled "The Substance and Structure of Network Television News: An Analysis of

Content Features, Format Features, and Formal Features." The author of that study examined numerous variables having to do with the newscasts of the three networks, including the frequency of occurrence of interviews. His sample consisted of 15 newscasts for each of the three networks, sampled in the period of January through June of 1973, that is, six months prior to the sample I have been working on. Schneider's sample, in addition to being 25% larger than mine, also spans a wider time period, which would be less influenced by chance or random fluctuations in the way news is presented.

Although the overall framework of Schneider's analysis is different and his definitions of the situation vary slightly, his findings are remarkably similar to mine. Schneider reports that the incidence of interviews in the CBS newscasts was 22.5%, it was 17.0% in the NBC newscasts, and 14.0% at ABC. In other words, this is comparable with my findings that CBS had more interviews per newscast (an average of 17.8), NBC came next with 15.3 interviews per newscast, and ABC with a mean of 9.8 had the fewest interviews per newscast. Moreover, Schneider found that the length of the average interview on the ABC newscasts was the longest and those of CBS were the shortest. As noted, my own findings also indicate that the average duration of the interview was longest in the ABC newscasts.

Thus despite the different measurement procedures and operational definitions used in the two studies, the findings in both cases indicate that there are indeed some differences among the three U.S. networks in the overall presence and use of interviews in the evening news. In a sense, Schneider's data provide a form of cross-validation to my findings (or perhaps vice versa) and, thereby, tend to negate the possibility that it was bias in the sampling framework that brought about the obtained differences. In other words, the three networks apparently did present different amounts of interviews in their newscasts. We shall discuss some of the possible meanings of this later on.

2. These findings are somewhat contradictory to the impressions reached by Gans (1979) in his study of the evening news at CBS and NBC (as well as at *Newsweek* and *Time*). Without providing empirical statistics, Gans reports that most of the people interviewed were in official capacities. He explains this by saying: "Rushed reporters do not have time to develop rapport with unfamiliar sources and go through the routines by which strangers become informants. Even when rapport in quickly attainable, as it is for television reporters whose cameras offer the promise of getting on the air, unfamiliar sources may provide information that cannot be assessed, thereby creating uncertainty" (pp. 139-140).

I would suggest that "in theory" Gans is probably correct. However, as the data seem to indicate, a significant number of "regular" people do appear as interviewees. This may also be an indication of some change in the pattern of news construction since Gans conducted his study in the late 1960s and early 1970s.

3. Throughout this study I have not resorted to statistical tests of significance in order to demonstrate the existence of differences among the networks (or among the countries in Chapter 5). This decision was made for three reasons: First, it is assumed that not all the readers of this book are sufficiently familiar with these concepts; second, there is increasing discussion in the methodological literature to cast some doubt on the use of test of significance; and third, and most important, what we are interested in is the substantive differences among the networks (and countries) and not whether or not they happen to be statistically significant. Incidentally, given the relatively large number of interviews analyzed, even a very small difference among the countries (or networks) is statistically significant anyway.

5

THE CROSS-NATIONAL COMPARISON

Data taken on the same night from Britain, West Germany, and Israel as well as from the United States indicate significant differences among the ways interviews in TV news are used in the various countries. This was the case for nearly all the variables examined.

The United States is not the only country that has television news and uses interviews and interviewers. How does the television news interview in the United States compare with that of other countries? It seems likely that cross-national comparisons will help toward a better fix on interviews in the United States; consequently this chapter presents more new information about television news interviews in Britain, West Germany, and Israel. Before looking at the data, however, here is a brief description of the television system in those countries that is directly pertinent to news.

Britain

Television broadcasting started in Britain in 1936. It began at the British Broadcasting Corporation (BBC) years after radio had been established as a major mass medium of communication. The BBC is government controlled and there is no advertising to interrupt its broadcasts. Thus the two television channels, BBC1 and BBC2, as they are called, are funded by the annual license fee that Britons are expected to pay (currently the fee is about the equivalent of $75 per year). Commercial television in Britain began in 1955 with the establishment of the Independent Broadcasting Authority (IBA), which administers Britain's two other channels. The third channel, called the Independent Television Network (ITV) is composed of several independent companies which produce programs for the ITV (some of the well-known companies are Thames, London Weekend and Granada). Recently, in 1983, a fourth channel was added, which is actually called Channel Four. It, too, is administered by the IBA. Thus there are presently four television channels in Britain: two noncommercial and two commercial. Recently, the Peacock Commission in Britain, which looked into the possibility of allowing the BBC to fund some of its activities by showing commercials, decided against this practice; hence the BBC will remain, at least for the time being, a noncommercial operation.

The news for the two BBC networks is produced by the BBC News Department, one of the world's most renowned news organizations. The news for the ITV and for Channel Four is produced by a subsidiary company of the IBA named Independent Television News (ITN). Both British networks have news correspondents stationed in many capitals of the world and in major trouble spots. In addition, the two networks are members of the European Broadcasting Union (EBU), which exchanges news items to and from its member countries via its News Exchange Service.

Each of the networks presents several newscasts every day: during the course of the early morning hours (which is a relatively new phenomenon in Britain), at around noon, and in the evening. The major newscasts are those in the evening hours. It should be noted that these broadcasts are shown relatively late in the evening (at 9 p.m. and at 10 p.m.). There are various formats of presentation, usually with one anchorperson, male or female, in the studio. There are several anchorpeople so that they rotate each evening. The British concept of "local" news is different from that in the United States. It comes in the form of "cut-ins" during Breakfast Television, for example, and has a purely local news/weather focus. Further, some of the IBA companies produce "local" news in the sense of regional (for instance, Midlands, Scotland) newcasts. The formats of these programs are very similar to the national news, not at all like the local news format in the United States.

West Germany

The first public broadcast of television in Germany took place in Berlin in March of 1935. During World War II these broadcasts were shut down and regular service was resumed in Hamburg on Christmas Day, 1952. Today there are two television networks in the Federal Republic of Germany (West Germany). The Federal Republic consists of a number of states, each is autonomous in cultural affairs and each supervises its own regional broadcasting stations. In the early 1950s, in order to promote the nationwide transmission of television programs, the stations embarked on a redevelopment policy, which created a merger into a federation called the ARD (which in German stands for the Standing Committes of Television Corporations of the Federal Republic of Germany). The ARD coordinates the work of nine regional corporations, based in such cities as Munich, Frankfurt, Hamburg, Berlin, and Cologne. Mounting pressure to set up another network, also in the form of a federation of the German states, led to the beginning of broadcasts in 1963 of the ZDF (which stands for the Second German Television). In Germany, too, there is a license fee to fund the operations of television, which is roughly the same as in Britain. Both networks, which operate under legal charters, are permitted to broadcast advertisements, but only the ZDF broadcasts commercials nationally, whereas the ARD does so on a regional basis.

There is one major evening newscast on each of the two networks that is transmitted nationally. There are also news programs of regional affairs, broadcast in the various states, but not at the more "intimate" level of the local news concept in the United States. The German networks also have correspondents in many places around the world and they, too, receive news items from the EBU news service to which they subscribe. Each evening newscast is anchored by one of several people, men and women, on a rotation basis.

Israel

There is only one television channel in Israel. It is state owned, and operated by the Israel Broadcasting Authority, which also runs Israel's radio services (in five channels). The television channel operates during most of the day, but it is shared by three separate programming systems. During the morning and afternoon hours the channel is used by the Instructional Television Center, which provides educational as well as cultural enrichment programs. In the early evening hours (from 6:30-8:00 p.m.) the channel is devoted to Arabic programs. The regular Hebrew broadcasts are on the air from 8:00 p.m. to around midnight. The major evening newscast is aired at 9 p.m. It generally runs for 30 minutes, but it is flexible and can go for up to one hour or more if some major news story has occurred. There is also a news summary at the end of the evening's broadcast, roughly around midnight.

About 50% of the programming for Israel Television is locally produced, and the other programs are imported, mainly from the United States and Britain. The Israeli system is also financed by an annual license fee. There are no "genuine" commercials on Israel Television, although there are numerous public service announcements that often border on commercial interests. Moreover, during the past year program sponsorship has become the "trick" to increase the station's revenue without showing bona fide commercials. In the realm of entertainment programs, Israel Television is in some competition with

Jordanian Television, Lebanese Television, and in some regions even Syrian television. This is due to the fact that these broadcasts can be picked up from across its borders and polls have shown that Israelis indeed watch television from their neighboring countries. However, as far as television news is concerned, the 9 p.m. newscast is very popular and is viewed each evening by about 85% of the adult population of the country. Despite its small size and relatively few viewers, Israel Television has correspondents in several foreign locations and it, too, is a member of the EBU and uses its news exchange quite frequently. The news is presented by a pair of anchors who sit side by side in the same studio. Usually both are male or one male and one female, although recently there have been occasions when two female newscasters presented the news. There is no concept of "local" news on Israel Television due to the small size of the country. (It is interesting to note that Israel Radio has a so-called special edition of local news, which consists of news items about various communities, often remote, but which is broadcast across the entire country for everyone to hear.)

THE CROSS-NATIONAL COMPARATIVE FRAMEWORK

The sample of the British news used in this study was that of BBC1's *News At Nine*. As I have just explained, however, there are several major newscasts each evening in Britain. Given budgetary restrictions, I analyzed the news of only one British network. The choice of BBC1 was based on the fact that it was, at the time of the data collection, the newscast viewed by more viewers than any other newscast. This selection could obviously bias the sample somewhat, but we had no alternative and this should be kept in mind when considering the results.

As for West Germany, a different kind of decision was necessary. Whereas in Britain, Israel, and the United States, the gross running time of the evening newscasts is roughly 30 minutes (with the exception of Britain's Channel Four *News At Ten*, which runs for one full hour), the two German networks carry significantly shorter newscasts. Thus the ARD's *Tageschau* (which means "the day's show") runs for roughly 20 minutes, while the ZDF's *Heute* (which means "today") generally runs for 15 minutes. Moreover, given our overall initial impression that German television newscasts have relatively few interviews (see the actual findings below) we felt that we should use the combined raw data from both newscasts, giving us about 35 minutes of news per evening.

The situation in Israel was the most simple by far in this regard. As there is only one television station in the country, we did not need to exercise any judgment in making our selection of *Mabat La' Hadashot* (which literally means "viewpoint on the news"). As indicated, it usually runs for 30 minutes, and sometimes more.

It seems, then, that the selection of the present sampling framework gives but a small clue to the complexity of doing cross-national research. The situation in the United States is ideal, of course, from the point of view of the researcher, as the three newscasts are exactly the same length, they are shown at the same time of day, and they are viewed by quite similar audiences. Thus for the purpose of the cross-national comparison I combined all of the 514 U.S. news items of the three U.S. networks. Of course, a difference of a few percentage points in the ratings is very significant from a commercial point of view, but not of major concern to media researchers unless the factor being studied, in this case, interviewing in the news, could be considered as the actual reason that brings about the difference in the audience share. Since this assumption is not being made here, this is not of any concern to us.

To recapitulate, then, the sample for the cross-national sample consists of 12 nights of the combined newscasts of the three U.S. networks, the one British program, the combined two West German newscasts, and the only existing Israeli news program. Needless to say, the difference in the number and length of the newscasts are taken into account in the statistical analyses which follow.

The order of presentation of the cross-national findings is the same as was the case in Chapter 4 when I discussed the three U.S. networks. Thus I shall commence with a general description of the interviews conducted in all four countries. This will be followed by specific findings concerning the identity variables, the situational variables, the verbal variables, and finally the nonverbal variables.

One brief point on the notations I shall be using in the tables. The British newscasts are identified by the abbreviation UK (United Kingdom); the West German newscasts by the abbreviation FRG (Federal Republic of Germany); I shall use ISR as an abbreviated form for the Israeli newscasts; and finally, of course, I shall identify the three U.S. networks with the abbreviation USA.

GENERAL CHARACTERISTICS OF THE
INTERVIEWS IN ALL FOUR COUNTRIES

Just as in Chapter 4, which dealt with the U.S. interviews, I was only interested in news items that contained interviews. In order to begin with the cross-national comparison, we must first provide some general information on the parameters of interviewing in the evening newscasts of the four countries that form the basis of the analyses. Table 1 presents this information.

The findings of Table 1 seem to suggest substantial differences between the four countries in terms of the prevalence of interviews in the news. However, in order to make a valid assessment of the differences, the data must be corrected for the different number of newscasts studied in each country.

Thus on the average, the U.S. networks had 17.0 news items per newscast, the British had 17.2 news items per newscast; the West German networks had an average of only 12.0 items per newscast (it should be recalled that each of their two newscasts is shorter in duration); and the Israeli newscasts consists of an average of 20.5 news items (as noted, the Israeli newscasts often run longer than the scheduled 30 minutes, which could explain this difference).

Overall, there are substantial differences in the percentages of news items containing at least one interview in each of the four countries. In the three U.S. networks 31% of all the news items contained at least one interview; in Britain 39% of the items contained at least one interview; in West Germany the respective figure is only 11%; and in Israel 28% of all the news items contained at least one interview. Thus the findings indicate that the smallest proportion of items containing interviews is in West Germany and the highest proportion is in Britain, the difference being about 3½ times. Another way of looking at the differences among the countries is by calculating the average number of interviews per newscast. Thus in the United States, on the average, each newscast contained 14.3 interviews; in Britain the average newscast contained 10.1 interviews; in West Germany there was only an average of 2.2 interviews per newscast; and in Israel there was an average of 11.0 interviews per newscasts. As for the mean number of interviews per newscasts which contains at least one interview, the findings are as follows: the U.S.—2.7 interviews per item; Britain—1.5 interviews per item; West Germany—1.7 interviews per item; and Israel—1.9 interviews per item. In other words, when considering only those items in the newscasts which contained interviewing, the U.S. networks tended to have nearly 3 interviews per item, whereas Britain had only a mean of 1½ interviews per item. Israel was relatively close to the United States, whereas West Germany was very similar to Britain. The relatively high number for West Germany is a statistical artifact: Since so few items have any interviews, the number of interviews in items containing at least one interview is relatively high.

TABLE 1
General Statistics on Television News Interviewing
in the Four Countries

	USA	UK	FRG	ISR
Number of news items	612	206	288	246
Overall number of interviews	514	121	53	132
Overall number of interview clips	657	131	55	151
Percentage of news items with at least one interview	31	39	11	28
Average number of interviews per story	2.7	1.5	1.7	1.9
Average length of interview (in seconds)	13.4	25.8	43.7	41.0
Range of interview length (in seconds)	1-142	5-118	4-201	3-390
Percentage of time devoted to interviews in newscast	14	17	9	22

As for the number of clips per interview, nearly 78% of the U.S. interviews consisted of one clip, in Britain 85% of the interviews consisted of one clip, in West Germany the respective figure was 93%, and in Israel 96% of the interviews had only one clip. As for the mean number of clips per interview, an interview in the U.S. newscasts contained an average of 1.28 clips; in Britain, the average was 1.08 clips per interview; in West Germany there were 1.04 clips per interview; and in Israel there was an average of 1.14 clips in each interview. As far as the length of the average interviews is concerned, the West German television news interviews were the longest, lasting nearly 44 seconds per interview, in Israel the average duration was 41 seconds, in Britain nearly 26 seconds long, and in the United States the average interview was only slightly over 13 seconds long. As for the range of the interviews, in all four countries there were very brief interviews lasting from one to five seconds (a one-second interview could be a one- or two-word statement, such as "I accept" or "Don't worry!"). However, the duration of the longest interviews varied from nearly 2 minutes in Britain to 6½ minutes in Israel. Finally, although the West German interviews were, on average, the longest of the four countries, since they were relatively infrequent, they took up only 9% of the entire newscasts. In the United States the respective figure was 14%, and in Britain 17%. In Israel, where there were relatively many interviews of long duration, all the interviewing took up over one-fifth of the newscasts (22%).

In summing up the findings to this point, it becomes clear that the differences between the networks in the four countries is considerably greater than the differences among the three U.S. networks, as reported in the previous chapter. Clearly the most salient finding is the relatively little use that the West German networks make of television news interviews. Thus in only 11% of their news items did interviews appear, on the average there were slightly more than 1½ interviews per item that contain any interviews, and yet when an interview was conducted it was relatively quite long, lasting on the average, nearly 44 seconds, and most of the interviews consisted of only one clip.

In Britain, on the other hand, we found that nearly 39% of all news items contain interviews, more than in any of the other countries. The news items containing interviews had an average of 1.5 interviews per item, the duration of each interview was moderate and stood at nearly 26 seconds, and 15% of the interviews had more than one clip.

In Israel, fewer items contain interviews (nearly 28% of all items) but on the average each item containing at least one interview actually had almost two interviews. The length of the average interview was almost as it was in West German (41 seconds), but Israel had several extremely long interviews, the longest lasting 6½ minutes, and 96% of its interviews consisted of one clip only.

Finally, in the United States, despite the fact that fewer items contained interviews (31%) as compared with Britain, the average number of interviews in the newscasts was the highest among the four countries with more than 14 interviews per newscast, and an average of almost three interviews were conducted per news item containing at least one interview. The average interview was the shortest, lasting about 13 seconds, and 22% of the interviews were presented with more than one clip.

Reducing the findings even further we can say that the United States and the British interviews on television news tend to be relatively frequent, short, with more clips and complex editing (taking into account the length of the interviews, there were more than double the number of cuts in the U.S. interviews compared with the other three countries). On the other hand, the West German interviewing was especially heavy with few and lengthy interviews and with most interviews done in one clip. The Israeli style of interviewing was somewhat in between, with relatively more frequent interviews but also relatively very lengthy ones.

THE VARIABLES EXAMINED

Let us now return to the format used when presenting the findings for the three U.S. networks. It will be recalled that the data were presented first for the identity code variables, followed by the variables dealing with the situational codes, and ending with the verbal and nonverbal code variables. Let us begin, then, with the identity codes of the interviews in Britain, West Germany, Israel and the United States.

Topics of Interview Items

The first of the identity variables is that of the topic of the news items in which the interviews appear. Table 2 presents the distribution of the interviews by the general topics of the items in all four countries of the study.

If we considered the differences found among the three U.S. networks as somewhat interesting, then by comparison the differences between the four countries could be characterized as overwhelming. On West German television, for example, 52% of all the interviews had to do with internal German politics; in the United States 19% of all the interviews were in this category; in Israel—9%; and, finally, Britain had only 5% of its interviews having to do with internal politics. Another example is internal order: In Britain 18% of the news items containing interviews were on this topic, in the United States 12%, in Israel 9%, and in West Germany no items on internal order containing interviews appeared at all. A final example is the case of news items concerning labor issues: In Britain 17% of all the interviews had to do with labor issues, in Israel 11% were on this topic, in West Germany 4%, and in the United States only 1% of the news items containing interviews dealt with labor issues.

Just as we have done for the U.S. networks, we need to compare the distribution of the topics of the items containing interviews with the general distribution of all the items in order to determine if interviewing is more prevalent in certain topics than in others. What we found is that for many of the entries in Table 2 there was a high degree of correspondence between the distribution of all the items according to the general topic categories and the distribution of only those items that contain at least one interview. However, there are some notable exceptions.

Thus as I indicated already in the previous chapter, in the United States only 3% of the news items were concerned with health and welfare, whereas 10% of the items with interviews dealt with health and welfare; also, less than 1% of the news items were sports items, but 4% of the interviews were in this category. On the other hand, 21% of all the items were concerned with international politics, whereas only 7% of the items with interviews dealt with international politics; similarly, whereas 13% of all the news items were business-related stories, only 6% of all the items with interviews were concerned with business.

TABLE 2
News Interviews by Topic Categories and Countries (in percentages)

Topics	USA (514)	UK (121)	FRG (53)	ISR (132)
Internal politics	19	5	52	9
Internal order	12	18	–	9
Human interest	11	6	–	2
Health and welfare	10	2	–	14
International politics	7	5	4	11
Economics	6	4	14	11
Business	6	11	15	8
Disasters and accidents	5	11	–	1
Defense	4	3	10	2
Sports	4	9	–	–
Education	3	1	–	10
Science and technology	3	3	–	–
Social relations	3	4	–	3
Labor	1	17	4	11
Others	6	1	1	9

In Britain there were three item categories in which there was overrepresentation of interviews. Thus while only 11% of all the items dealt with labor issues, 17% of all the items with interview were on the labor front; also, while 5% of the items were concerned with business activities, 11% of the interview items were in this category; and finally, while only 6% of the items presented accidents and disasters, 11% of all the items with interviews were with people involved with accidents and disasters. On the other hand, underrepresentation of interviews was found among items on internal politics as well as on international politics items: Both these categories of news stories composed 13% of all the news items, but of all the interview items only 5% appeared in each of them.

In West Germany there were only 29% of items dealing with internal politics but 52% of all the interview items were in this category; 7% of the stories were on economic matters but 14% of the interviews were on that subject; 4% of the items were on business matters with 15% of all the interview items on that topic; and 3% of the items were in the defense arena but 10% of all the interviews were on that topic. On the other hand, several categories in West German television were underrepresented in terms of interviewing: Internal order items represented 10% of all the items but there were no interviews in those items; international politics represented 23% of all the items, but among the interview items there were only 4% on international politics; finally, 4% of the items were concerned with human relations and an additional 4% were human interest stories, but none of the stories in either category had even a single interview.

As for Israel, only 3% of all the news items were in the field of education, but 10% of all the interview items were of that category; also, 5% of the items dealt with health and welfare but as many as 14% of the interview items were on that topic. On the other hand, the area of internal politics had 14% of all the items, but only 9% of the interview items; similarly, internal order items made up 17% of all the items but were only represented in 9% of the interview items; and finally, international politics stories represented 18% of all the news items but only 11% of the interview items.

Looking across all four countries, two trends seem to appear. First, news items concerning international politics, which are heavily evident in all the newscasts, are highly underrepresented as far as interviewing is concerned. This may be due either to the relative difficulty to obtain interviews, particularly with people from foreign countries (despite the availability of satellites and other technological devices) or to the fact that such matters are more concerned with institutions rather than with individual human beings. Also, there is a tendency for items on economics (in West Germany and Israel), business (in Britain, West Germany, and Israel) and labor (in Britain) to have relatively more interviews than their general proportion in the entire array of topics. This may be due to the fact that such topics are relevant to individual people as workers or consumers. In addition, in West Germany and Israel there are fewer interviews concerning internal order than would be expected based on the number of such news items in the newscasts. Finally, there is relatively more interviewing than would be expected by the overall distribution of topics regarding health and welfare in the United States and concerning education in Israel. These topics also concern individual people and may be the reason for their relatively high salience in the context of interviewing.

Interviews in Social Conflict Items

Just as we have found for the three U.S. networks, so with the other three countries it seems that social conflict is highly represented in the news items that contain interviews. Thus in Britain 39% of all the items contained social conflict but 52% of all the items with interviews contained social conflict. In West Germany the figures are 56% and 72%, respectively, and in Israel 61% of all the items contained social conflict and 63% of the interview items contained social conflict. Just as a reminder, in the United States the overall respective figures were 50% and 55%.

This seems to reinforce the notion suggested earlier that interviewing is more likely to take place in news items that contain social conflict compared with items that are not concerned with social conflict. This is probably because of the fact that controversy among conflicting parties presents potentially good material for television reporters in their attempt to present drame and excitement.

Language of the Interview

Whereas in the case of the three U.S. networks 99% of the interviews were conducted in their native language, that is, in English, the situation is somewhat different in the other countries studied. In Britain only 2.5% of the interviews were conducted with people in a language other than English, but in West Germany and in Israel 15% of all the interviews were conducted in a language other than German and Hebrew, respectively.

Of the five non-English interviews in the U.S. networks, four had voice-over translation into English and one had no translation at all. In Britain, of the three non-English interviews one had voice-over translation and the other two were not translated. In West Germany, the eight non-German interviews were all translated into German using voice-over. Finally, in Israel, the 20 non-Hebrew interviews were translated into Hebrew using subtitles on the screen. In other words, only in Israel were the news viewers able actually to hear interviews in nonnative languages, and they were able to read the translations, if they so wished.

Gender and Role of Interviewers

As with the case of the U.S. networks, so with the non-U.S. interviewers, we wanted to determine the specific identity of the interviewer. Often it was necessary to determine the identity of the person conducting the interview by his or her visual presence or voice unless some specific references are made to the interviewer, such as "our correspondent John Doe asked (or spoke with) Mr. Smith." Nevertheless there were numerous cases in which a precise determination was impossible as the interviewer was not seen or heard in the course of the interview. This, of course, is interesting information in and of itself, as we are talking about interviews that are conceptually defined as a conversation between two persons (or more) aimed at extracting information.

In any event, in the United States, as indicated, in 60% of the cases it was impossible to determine who the interviewer was. In Britain it was impossible to make the determination in 43% of the cases, in West Germany in 23% of the cases, and in Israel only 8% of the cases, that is, the interviewer was present in Israel in 92% of the interviews.

In the United States the correspondent was seen or heard in 34% of the interviews; in Britain in 50%, in West Germany in 76%, and in Israel in 89% of the interviews. In addition, the anchor person in the United States conducted the interviews in 1.4% of the cases and in Israel in 3% of the cases. In Britain and in West Germany the anchor person did not conduct any of the interviews.

Even the gender of the interviewer was not always determinable based on the necessary audio and/or visual cues. Thus in the United States, in 58% of the cases it was impossible to say who the interviewer was, in Britain it was impossible in 42% of the cases, in West Germany in 19% of the cases, and in Israel in 2% of the cases. Note that these percentages are, of course, lower in all the countries than the total absence of cues.

When it was possible to determine the gender of the interviewer, it was found that only in 4% of the cases in the United States was the interviewer a woman, in Britain no women did any of the interviews, in West Germany only one interview was conducted by a woman, and in Israel four interviews (or 3% of the cases) were interviewed by a woman.

Role Characteristics of the Interviewees

As with the U.S. networks, three kinds of characteristics of the interviewees were presented—first, the gender of the interviewees; next, the frequency of native interviewees, that is, people from the country of broadcast; and finally, the roles and social positions of the interviewees. All these data are presented for the four countries in Table 3.

As for the gender of the interviewees, it seems that in West Germany nearly all the interviewees were men, whereas in the other three countries 16%-17% of all the interviewees were women.

Concerning the question of being a native of the country in which the interview is presented, in the two English speaking countries only 5%-8% of the interviewees were foreigners, whereas in Israel and in West Germany there were more foreign interviewees, ranging from 15% to 17%, respectively.

Regarding the social roles that the interviewees fulfill in their respective societies, there seems to be a complex, albeit interesting picture. As for interviewees defined as public officials, in West Germany

TABLE 3
Summary of Identity Variables of the Interviewees
by Country (in percentages)

	USA (514)	UK (121)	FRG (53)	ISR (132)
Gender of interviewee (male)	83	83	93	84
Native to country of broadcast	95	92	83	85
Public official	37	31	74	49
Elected to position	28	22	53	30
Professional/expert	42	41	40	21
Random selection	44	34	25	32
Victim	24	25	19	35
Involved	86	94	81	97

an overwhelming majority (74%) were of that social category, in Israel the corresponding figure was 49%, and in Britain and the United States they were 31% and 37%, respectively.

As for being elected to one's position, in West Germany 53% of all the interviewees were persons elected to their respective positions, whereas in the other three countries there were only between 22% and 30% of the interviewees who were elected officials.

Being a professional or expert in the field with which the interview is concerned presents yet a different picture. In Israel the percentage of expert or professional interviewees stood at 21%, whereas in the other countries this figure ranged from 40% to 42%.

The use of a "random" choice for the interviewee also varies among the four countries. In West Germany there were the fewest randomly selected interviewees (25%), whereas the highest proportion of randomly selected interviewees was in the United States (44% of all the interviewees). Israel and Britain were in between with 32% and 34%, respectively.

The frequency of the interviewee being a "victim" in the story being reported is also different in the countries examined. In Israel 35% of all the interviewees were "victims" of one kind or another in the context of the news event being reported; in the United States and Britain 24%-25% of the interviewees were victims, and in West Germany only 19% of all the interviewees were victims.

The final role examined was that of being "involved" in the story being reported. In Israel nearly all (97%) of the interviewees were involved in the stories in which they were interviewed, in Britain this was the case in 94% of the cases, in the United States in 86%, and in West

Germany only 81% of all the interviewees were involved. Put differently, 19% of all the West German interviewees were not involved in the stories in which they were interviewed.

Explicit Identification of the Interviewees

As with the three U.S. networks, we checked the use of the captions identifying the interviewees and also of verbal references made to them. In the United States, in 37% of the interviews there was absolutely no reference made to the interviewee, neither in printed captions nor verbally. In Britain no references were made in 60% of the interview items, in West Germany in 19%, and in Israel in 28% of the cases.

The use of printed captions only, that is, without any verbal identification of the interviewee, was used in the United States in 44% of the cases, in Britain in 28%, in West Germany in 38%, and in Israel in 63% of all the interviews.

Finally, the combined use of both verbal references and visual captions was employed in West Germany in 36% of the cases, and in the other three countries from 6% to 9% of the cases.

The average amount of time during which visual captions identifying the interviewee were on the screen was 1.8 seconds in the United States, 2.3 seconds in Israel, 3.0 seconds in Britain, and 4.3 seconds in West Germany.

SITUATIONAL VARIABLES

The second set of variables examined in the cross-cultural analysis have to do with the situation or the general context of the interview. The four situational variable studied were the location and the physical background of the interviews, the directness of the broadcast, and the use of editing.

The Location of the Interview

Of all the interviews conducted in Britain, 84% were conducted on location and 13% were conducted in the news studio with both the interviewer and interviewee present (it was impossible to determine the location of 3% of the interviews). In West Germany, 89% of the interviews were conducted on location, 8% were conducted in the studio, and the location of 3% of the interviews was impossible to determine. In Israel 96% of the interviews were conducted on location, 2% in the studio, and 2% in unknown locations. Finally, as indicated earlier, in the United States, 96% of the interviews were conducted on location, 2% in the studio, and in 2% of the cases the location was impossible to tell.

The Background of the Interview

The settings in which the interviews of the four countries were conducted are presented in Table 4.

As can be seen, there are some impressive differences among the four countries. In the United States the most commonly used background for an interview on television news was in an office setting, followed by a public place such as a store, a street, a public (nongovernmental) building, and so on. Besides the studio setting, the least number of interviews were conducted in government buildings. In Britain, the most popular place for the news interviews was a public place followed by an office setting. Also, in Britain, as in the United States, the fewest interviews took place in government buildings. In West Germany, on the other hand, the greatest number of interviews took place in government buildings followed by public places, with offices far behind in third place. The fewest interviews took place in the home setting. And in Israel, the greatest number of interviews took place in public places followed by general places of work and government buildings close behind. As in Germany, the fewest number of interviews took place in a home setting.

Live Versus Prerecorded and Edited Interviews

Comparing the four countries on this variable indicates that Israel is clearly different from the other three: 7.6% of all the interviews in Israel were conducted "live," with less than 1% in Britain and 1.6% in the United States. In West Germany not a single interview was conducted in a "live" situation.

VERBAL VARIABLES

As stated earlier, the verbal codes have to do with the interaction during the interview, that is, the questioning techniques and the rules of etiquette practiced by the reporters and the interviewees. As in the case of the U.S. networks, I present the findings from the four countries separately for the interviewer and the interviewee. Let us begin with the interviewer.

TABLE 4
Locations of the Interviews by Country (in percentages)

	USA (514)	UK (121)	FRG (53)	ISR (132)
General place of work	10	14	2	21
Clearly visible office	30	16	13	14
Nature (out-of-doors)	11	12	–	8
Government building	6	1	34	20
At home	7	12	2	–
Public place	24	24	32	26
Studio	2	14	6	5
Could not be determined	10	7	11	5

Number of Questions Heard

The use of questions by the interviewer is probably the best measure of the interaction between the interviewer and the interviewee. As indicated earlier, in the U.S. interviews a total of 74 questions were heard, which is an average of 0.14 questions per interview. In the other countries the situation in this respect is quite different.

In Britain a total of 90 questions were heard being put to the interviewees, for an average of 0.74 questions per interview. In Israel a total of 111 questions were heard, which represent an average of 0.84 questions per interview. And in West Germany only 72 questions were heard, but given the relatively few number of interviews, the mean number of questions per interview was a very high 1.36, in other words, on the average, each interview on West German television news contained nearly 1½ questions that could be heard by the audience. Looking at this data in a slightly different perspective, in 91% of the U.S. interviews not a single question was heard. In Britain the comparable figure was 65%, in Israel 64%, and in West Germany only 36%.

Repeated and Provocative Questions and Interruptions

Regarding the repeated questions put to the interviewees, as indicated in the U.S. networks there were only three such questions which represent 4% of all the 74 questions heard. In Britain 4 repeated questions were heard which represent 8% of all the 90 questions asked, in West Germany 3 repeated questions were asked which represent 4% of the 72 questions asked, and in Israel 10 repeated questions were asked and heard which represent 9% of the 111 questions asked.

The use of provocative questions was also examined in the cross-national context. It will be recalled that in the U.S. interviews, of the 74 questions heard, 18 (or 24%) were coded as provocative. In the other countries the findings are as follows: In West Germany, 4 of the 72 questions (6%) were considered by the coders to be provocative; in Britain 12 of the 90 (13%) were scored as being provocative; and in Israel 15 of the 111 questions (14%) were determined to be provocative.

As for interruptions of the interviewee by the interviewer, as noted, in the United States this phenomenon was quite rare, occurring in less than 1% of the interviews. In West Germany this occurred three times, which represents nearly 6% of the interviews, in Britain there were six interruptions, which means it happened in 5% of the interviews, and in Israel there were 16 cases of the interviewer interrupting the interviewee, that is, this happened in 12% of the interviews.

Verbal Presence of the Interviewer

The most dominant person heard and seen in the interview is the interviewee. However, the interviewer is also heard and seen at certain points in the interview. An analysis of the audio presence of the reporter, including asking the questions, in the interviews of the four countries reveals substantial differences. The average presence of the U.S. interviewers was 0.81 seconds per interview, in Britain it was 2.21 seconds per interview, in West Germany 6.52 seconds per interview, and in Israel 2.26 seconds per interview. Put in another way, in the United States, the interviewers were heard during 6% of the total interviewing time, in Britain the interviewers were heard during 9% of the interviewing time, in West Germany they were heard during 15% of the total interviewing time, and in Israel the interviewers were heard during 6% of the total interviewing time.

The Use of First Names by the Interviewer

The use of first names by the interviewer was found in only two Israeli interviews and in eight of the U.S. interviews. In West Germany there was not a single case of either participant in the interview using the first name of the other person; and in Britain there was one case in which both participants used each other's first name.

The Use of First Names by the Interviewee

Of all the 820 interviews analyzed, in only two cases in the United States was there a situation in which the interviewee referred to the interviewer by his first name. Also, the cases of reciprocal first name use, mentioned above, should be mentioned here as well, namely, the three U.S. cases and the one in Britain in which both participants referred to each other by their first names.

Role Switching

As for role switching, that is, the situation in which the interviewee turns to the interviewer to ask him or her a question, there were no such cases in Israel, there were six in Britain, one in West Germany, and five in the United States. It should be noted, however, that nearly all the cases of role switching in each of the countries occurred in one interview.

Verbal Presence of the Interviewee

The amount of time that the interviewees were heard talking during the course of the complete interviews were as follows: in the United States the average was 11.3 seconds, in Britain 21.0 seconds, in West Germany 40.0 seconds, and in Israel 35.4 seconds. This represents the following proportions of the complete length of the interviews: 90% in the United States, 88% in Britain, 85% in West Germany, and 92% in Israel.

Note that if one combines the time the interviewer and interviewee are both heard, the result does not always reach 100% of the time (in the United States, Britain, and Israel). This is because during brief segments of the interview there is silence and neither of the participants is heard talking. Looking at the overall statistics, however, this does not occur in Germany, that is, in the West German interviews, on the average, there are no periods of silence in the interviews.

NONVERBAL VARIABLES

Three measures of the nonverbal aspects of the interview are presented here: the spatial-physical arrangement, the use of microphones, and the framing of the interviewee in the picture.

Spatial-Physical Arrangement

The spatial-physical measures examined were the distance between the participants of the interviews and the posture of the interviewee. In Britain, in 7% of the interviews the participants were clearly close to one another, in 12% they were at a medium distance, in 3% they were far away, and in 78% of the cases it was impossible to tell. In 52% of the interviews the interviewees were sitting, in 43% they were standing, in 1% they were in motion, and in 4% it was impossible to determine.

In West Germany, in 66% of the interviews the participants were close to one another, in 8% they were at a medium distance from each other, and in 26% it was impossible to tell. In 17% of the interviews it was clear that the interviewees were sitting, in 72% of the cases they were standing, and in 11% of the interviews they were in motion.

In Israel, in 12% of the interviews the participants were definitely close to each other, in 14% they were at a medium distance, in 2% they were far from one another, and in 72% it was impossible to tell. In 27% of the Israeli interviews the interviewees were sitting, in 67% they were standing, in 1% they were in motion, and in 5% it was impossible to tell.

Finally, in the United States, as we saw in the previous chapter, in 22% of the interviews (across the three networks) the participants were close to one another, in 25% they were at a medium distance from each other, in 2% they were far from each other, and in 51% it was impossible to tell how far they were from each other. Also, in 47% of the cases the interviewee was sitting, in 42% he or she was standing, in 1% there was motion, in 1% of the cases the interviewee was in a reclining position, and in 9% of the interviews it was impossible to tell the posture of the interviewee.

The Kind of Microphone Used

The determination of the kind of microphone used was based on the visual cues that were available in the frame of the picture as seen on the screen. Table 5 presents the findings on the use of the microphone during the interviews.

In the United States, Britain, and Israel it was impossible to determine the kind of microphone used in 84%, 79%, and 82% of the cases, respectively. However, in West Germany in only 36% of the interviews it was not possible to determine the kind of microphone being used.

TABLE 5
Use of Microphones by Country (in percentages)

	USA (514)	UK (121)	FRG (53)	ISR (132)
Lavalier	8	7	2	2
Hand-held	7	9	59	8
Soundman, table mike	1	5	3	8
Cannot determine	84	79	36	82

In the United States and in Britain the lavalier-type microphone was definitely used in 7%-8% of the cases (although it is most likely that they were used in many more cases that could not be detected visually on the screen, due to the framing of the shot of the interviewee). In West Germany and in Israel the lavalier could be seen in only 2% of the cases.

However, the most salient difference was the use of the hand microphone held by the reporter-interviewer. In West Germany this kind of microphone was visibly seen in 59% of the interviews, whereas in the other countries the hand mike could be seen in only 7%-9% of the cases. Other kinds of microphones (for instance, boom mikes, sound-men holding shotgun mikes, and so on) could be seen being used in relatively few cases (1% in the United States, 3% in West Germany, 5% in Britain, and 8% in Israel).

Visual Presence and the Framing of the Interviewee

In absolute terms, the mean amount of time that the interviewee was seen on the screen in the three U.S. networks was 12.4 seconds, in Britain the mean was 23.6 seconds, in West Germany 41.7 seconds, and in Israel the interviewee was seen on the average for 36.0 seconds. However, in relative terms, the amount of time that the interviewees were seen in the four countries are very similar. In other words, the U.S. interviewees were seen during 95% of the interviewing time, in Britain they were seen during 93% of the interview time, in West Germany for 95% of the time, and in Israel the interviewees were seen on the screen during 97% of the interviewing time.

As for the breakdown by the kind of visual shot being used (that is, medium shot, close-up, or extreme close-up), the proportion of time during which the interviewees were seen in each shot are presented in Table 6.

In three countries except for the United States, the interviewee is seen for most of the interview in a medium shot (ranging from 52% of the time in West Germany to 65% of the time in Britain). In the United States a medium shot is used only during an average of 24% of the time of the interview. On the other hand, in the United States there is a significant use of close-up shots (65% of the time of the interview) followed by Israel with 38% of the time, with Britain and West Germany ranging from 25% to 29%. Extreme close-up shots (from the chin to the forehead) are used rarely.

As we did in the previous chapter for the U.S. networks, let us now look at the measures of visual and audio presence of the interviewer

TABLE 6

The Interviewee Seen by Type of Shot and Country (in percentages)

	USA (514)	UK (121)	FRG (53)	ISR (132)
Medium shot	24	65	52	56
Close-up shot	65	25	29	38
Extreme close-up shot	4	2	5	1

during the interviews in all the countries. The average amount of time per interview that the interviewer was seen on the screen was 1.01 seconds in the U.S. networks combined, it was 0.82 seconds in Britain, 1.96 seconds in Israel, and 9.02 seconds in West Germany.

If one looks at the overall relationship between the visual and audio presence of the interviewer it becomes evident that in Britain and in Israel there is more time during which the interviewer is heard than he or she is seen, whereas in the United States and Germany the interviewer is seen on the average for more time than he or she is heard. This indicates that in the former two countries there is a greater tendency to show the *interviewee* while the question is being put to him or her by the interviewer, whereas in the latter two countries when the interviewer speaks it is he or she who is usually shown talking.

CONCLUSION

The findings of the cross-national comparison clearly indicate that on many variables there are distinct differences among the four countries, although this is not the case for all of the variables. Moreover, and what is more important, the patterns of differences are not the same across all the variables. Thus our next task is to attempt to integrate all the empirical findings and to suggest a satisfactory explanation for the differences found. This will be done in the following chapters.

6

INTERVIEWING THE INTERVIEWERS: WHAT REPORTERS SAY

In order to obtain another perspective and deeper understanding of the various countries, interviews were conducted with news anchors and reporters who actually do the interviewing. The reporters explained why they do things as they do and what implications this has for the news in their respective countries.

What should be very clear from the findings is that on some of the variables there seems to be a great deal of similarity among the three networks in the United States (Chapter 4) and among the four countries (Chapter 5). On the other hand, on some of the variables differences were found. Assuming, as I did, that television news reporters in the U.S. networks as well as in the other three countries share many professional norms and values on what television news should be like, and assuming that these norms and values are central to the news production process, this should have resulted in similarities among the networks and the countries in terms of how interviews are done. On the other hand, it should be clear that not only professional norms and values determine the way journalists operate and what their product looks like. Thus various social, political, and technological factors as well as idiosyncratic elements can influence how the reporters perform their work and produce the news.

One way to try to decipher the meaning of the differences is to consult the literature on television news. This literature, which is mainly sociological in its orientation (for instance, Epstein, 1973; Tuchman, 1978; Gans, 1979), discusses the professional values and norms at great length but gives relatively little attention to the news interview. Also, there is almost no available empirical research of a cross-cultural nature on the work of television journalists (with the recent exception by Kocher, 1986, which compares British and German journalists). In addition, as noted earlier, the professional nonacademic literature is quite meager, and does not even suggest what seem to be useful cues. Another approach is to use whatever information is available about the social, political, and technological aspects of the networks and the countries to try to understand the differences obtained. This method can definitely yield some insight into the problem, and I will turn to this later. Finally, it occurred to me that one viable approach would be to ask the reporters themselves. In other words, if the reporters do the interviewing, they presumably have some idea of why they do it the way they do, and why the final product appears as it does. This does not mean that they think about it every day and they are necessarily concerned about it, but if prompted to talk about it, they might be able to tell us something about the philosophy, the strategy, and the tactics they employ when they set out to do an interview and to prepare it for the newscast.

Therefore I interviewed some key people who conduct television news interviews as part of their normal work. I did this in the four countries of the study, and in the three U.S. networks. I spoke to more than 20 people, some of whom are active reporters, some of whom are television news anchors, and some of whom are involved in the production of television news after having spent many years as reporters. In order to do the interviews, I contacted, made appointments with those who were willing to speak to me, and then traveled to the United States, to Britain and to West Germany (I reside in Israel).

The interviews were semistructured, that is, I always began with a set of questions I had prepared and had intended to ask each of my respondents. However, most of the interviews quickly assumed the form of a conversation, in which I raised the various points in the order and context best suited in each individual interview.

I want to stress that under no circumstances do I consider my respondents as a representative sample of all television reporters and interviewers. I did attempt to interview a variety of people in terms of the networks they represented as well as the kind of positions they held (not only reporters but also news editors and producers) and the experience they had.

In the United States I spoke to the following people: Tom Brokaw, the anchor of *NBC Nightly News*; Lou Cioffi, ABC's United Nations Bureau Chief; Martin Fletcher, NBC's correspondent stationed in Israel; David Gelber, one of the producers of the *CBS Evening News* (who had just moved to *60 Minutes*); Mike Jensen, NBC's Chief Financial Correspondent; and Lynn Sherr, ABC's reporter on science who had just returned from an assignment in Africa.

In Britain, it will be recalled, I only did an analysis of one of the BBC's newscasts. And yet, I decided to attempt to speak with news interviewers at Independent Television News (ITN), the other news organization in the country, as well as to people at the BBC. The British list includes: Christopher Lowe, one of the BBC's reporters who also anchors the midday news; Leonard Parkin, the anchor of the ITN's *News At One*; Robin Paxton, Deputy Editor of *Weekend World,* London Weekend Television's talk show, which deals mainly with political and social issues; Andrew Taylor, a reporter with the BBC, Hugh Whitcomb, the Managing Editor of the ITN; Richard Whitmore, one of the BBC correspondents; and James Wilkinson, Science Correspondent of the BBC.

In West Germany I spoke to people at the country's two networks: Ralf-Eric Berg of the ZDF, who specializes in international affairs; Gerd Helbich, a reporter for the ZDF, who had a long record of overseas service; Peter Martin, the political correspondent of the ARD in Bonn; Hans Scheicher, the political correspondent of the ZDF in Mainz; and Friedrich Nowottny, the chief political reporter of the ARD, who was soon to assume the position of the commissioner of the ARD.

In Isreal I spoke to four people at Israel Television: Victor Nahmias, an Arab affairs specialist and correspondent; Yoram Ronen, the political correspondent of Israel Television; David Witzthum, who was serving at the time as Israel Television's correspondent in Western Europe (I interviewed him in Bonn, Germany); and Haim Yavin, news editor and the main anchor of the nightly news, who recently became head of Israel Television.

In the United States, I also spoke to three local television reporters, in an attempt to learn a bit more about the way local news people consider the interviewing on the national news. I chose the three news anchors at the three affiliated network stations in Buffalo, New York (simply because I spent a summer there). I spoke with Rich Kellman, one of NBC's anchor people in Buffalo; Rich Newberg, CBS's anchor on the weekend news; and Irv Weinstein, one of the main anchor people at the ABC affiliated station in Buffalo. It should be stressed that these people are affiliates of the networks but don't work directly for the networks.

All my conversations were recorded on tape, with the permission of the interviewees (yes, I was the interviewer this time and the reporters were my interviewees). I promised them, in return, not to identify them specifically when I quoted what they had to say. I felt that this was necessary in order to encourage them to make the most frank comments and observations. Therefore, when I refer to what a particular person said, I will only mention his or her nationality (after all, I am not really concerned, nor should the readers be, with the specific person or his or her station).

Finally, I shall present only excerpts of what the interviewees told me. I shall try to keep the remarks and citations as closely as possible within the context in which they were said. However, I shall not keep to the exact order of the more systematic presentation of the empirical findings of the content analysis. Instead, I shall try to present a coherent picture based on many hours of tapes and more than 100 pages of notes.

THE GREATEST COMPLAINT: LACK OF TIME

In the previous two chapters we have seen that there is great variability in the extent to which interviews are used in the newscasts and the length of television news interviews, particularly among the different countries. Therefore, I began each interview with the general question: "Are you satisfied with the way interviewing is conducted in television news?" Some of the reporters expressed a great measure of dissatisfaction while others noted a more mixed feeling. Few said they were totally satisfied with the present state of affairs. One interesting distinction did come out in a few of the interviews, namely, the gap between the methods employed in the interview and the product seen on the screen. Two U.S. reporters put it in quite similar terms: "The problem is not how an interview is done but what you get to use," and "I'm satisfied with the techniques that are used for the most part, but not satisfied with the way the product comes out."

When probed further about this (and even without probing) the general consensus seemed to be that not enough time is devoted to interviewing. Interviewing was perceived by many as a very difficult task, mainly with respect to the need to edit down the material into very brief segments. This idea was expressed by almost all the reporters, regardless of how long the typical interview was in their respective countries. One of the Germans put it in the most extreme terms: "Too little time, 90 seconds, three questions, three answers, the best is if you have five or six or seven minutes!" An Israeli reporter said: "Even if the interviewee is relaxed and intense, you cannot ask more than 3-4 questions in the time allotted." A British reporter told me: "You talk for 3-4 minutes, edit it down to 30-40 seconds, you need one clip which makes it even more difficult." And in the United States several reporters remarked: "Shorthanding is the hardest problem we have; I don't have a problem with how questions are asked but when you have good material the interviewee cannot have enough time to explain him/herself," and "The sound bite is a technique to get the person to wrap up his feelings in 15-20 seconds which is not always possible."

PRERECORDING AND EDITING INTERVIEWS

Among other things, the shortage of time is a function of the need to edit the interview. Given the fact that most national news interviews in the United States and in Germany, and to some extent in Britain, with the exception of Israel, are rarely done live, I asked the reporters and anchors what they thought about this possibility. The reasons were varied, and often not in accordance with the way things really are in the different countries.

One veteran U.S. reporter exclaimed: "Live! Live! Live! There's something about a reporter, a broadcast journalist, something about going live. That's the most exhilarating thing in the world, you know you really can't make a mistake, you really can't stumble, and its the most effective TV journalism there is." But he then continued: "You have less control this way, because you get one of those long winded people and ask them any question you want and he'll go off and answer three different questions, and you don't have time for that!" Another reporter from the same network said: "Oh yes, I'd rather do live TV than anything in the world; you get to say full sentences, you get to laugh, to express surprise, it's what the public wants to see, and I wish we could do more of it." In fact, I was told that there is a growing tendency in the U.S. network news to do live interviews from time to time.

In Germany, there seems to be some mixed feelings on the topic. Some reporters would definitely like to have live interviews, despite the fact that this hardly ever occurs in reality. One respondent said to me: "Most are edited, but if you're lucky it can be live. The ideal is live. It's the best situation for both reporter and interviewee. You must behave yourself, bring your brain together, to be concentrated." Another reported told me, however, "We never have a live interview on *Heute;* it would create a sensation; our news is more or less sterile, we're not lively enough, it is part of German character, we want to have serious news and serious people." Another reporter made this comment: "I would prefer the recording so I don't feel overpowered by my partner. It will give me a chance to do some editing, but normally live interviewing is better. Even if I do a recording I prefer the first take because you never get the reaction twice. We sometimes have interviewees who say after the interview 'this and this and this I don't want you to use!' We should forget about this person."

In Britain, on the other hand, several of my interviewees felt that edited interviews should be preferred, in most cases. One British producer said: "On balance, edited! We have four different programs each day; lunch time (*News At One*) has more live. Historically, by noon we didn't have enough time to get filmed materials, we went for live; it does have a certain impact, being live, but we prefer prerecorded and edited." Two British reporters were also quite reserved on the topic: "Live? Maybe one per program, but edited is more efficient. Very rare to have live on *BBC At Nine*" and "depends on the story, if it's big enough, the miners' strike for example, they happened occasionally, not often, they are rare but possible." Another reporter was even more adamant: "No, unless it's terribly important. It's a terrible waste of air-time. It was terrible during the Falkland War that we went live each night to MacDonald who gave the briefings. It was nerve racking because we didn't know what he was going to say, but it was taking five minutes of air-time. It's cheap and it fills up time, that's maybe why they do it. On the lunch-time news it's OK, but not at *News At Nine*."

In Israel there were mixed feelings among my interviewees. One reporter said: "Live, of course! The interviewee is more tense, but the disadvantage is that you often cannot manage within the time slot that you are given." One of his colleagues said, "It's hard to say, in the live interview there is more drama, there is a real person out there, one cannot evade the question, but the recording also has its advantages. In sum I guess I prefer the pre-recorded version."

The prerecorded interview entails various editing problems. The reporters were also asked about this. It seems that in Germany this issue was put in the most concise terms by one of the reporters I spoke to: "The problem in Germany is that we are reluctant to edit interviews. We more or less do an interview and take it as it is. I have an example—I was going to do an interview with the Shah of Iran and he asked me: 'Are you going to do it the American way or are you doing an interview and take it as it is?' Another example—a few days ago Mr. Kohl was interviewed. At the end we always say—'Mr. Chancellor, Thank you very much!' but edit this out. By mistake, the 'Mr. Chancellor' stayed in. We imme-diately got many calls asking us what question was left out. They suspected a manipulation." Another German described the editing dilemma this way: "Time is a big factor. If you place a question the politician begins to think 'out loud.' Thinking can be taken out and we can just use his direct answer. We take out the 'blah, blah' as we call it." Finally, another German reporter told me: "I try to get the interview shortened by taking out a whole part. I consult with the politician—he has to be informed. It's not just a question of politeness, it's the normal way to deal with contents."

The British and Israeli reporters, when asked about editing pro-cedures, simply said that they look for the "best" or most "interesting" piece to put into their package. One of the U.S. reporters, however, made what I thought was quite a revealing admission: "The problem is that when we begin an interview we know what we want out of it; we know what to expect; we know what sound bite we want, more or less, and often go for that sound bite; we know what we expect him to say, that's why we've chosen him . . . when he says what we are looking for, that's when the interview is over." I presented this notion to some of the other U.S. interviewers and they tended to agree. As one put it: "That is probably more candor than the others will permit themselves. My guess is that in a produced story that is what's happening." Another reporter disagreed, however: "After the interviewee talks a lot, I may ask him to put it in a 15-second clip, but I won't lead him to say what I want him to say. In hard news you don't have time for this."

LIVE INTERVIEWS IN THE NEWS STUDIO

The live interview with a person in the news conducted in the news studio is a special kind of situation. I asked the reporters about their feelings concerning this format. In doing so I suggested to them the metaphor of the interviewee who enters the studio and sits next to the anchor as an "invader" of the "holiest of holy" places—where traditionally only the high priest (and analogously the news anchor) may enter.

In Britain there seemed to be mixed feelings about this practice. One reporter said, "No, unless it's terribly important." His colleague disputed this, however: "Sometimes it's essential in the studio, on major occasions like for the P.M.'s [Prime Minister's] first 100 days. We would prefer the setting at 10 Downing Street, but we have no aversion against the studio when it seems to be appropriate."

One of the U.S. reporters said, "Generally people feel more relaxed in their own environment, but I would prefer to bring the people into the studio than to do a live remote interview."

In Israel, where live in-studio interviews often take place, one of the reporters said, "I actually prefer the live interview from the field, let's say directly from the Prime Minister's office and not from the studio, but it doesn't really bother me to do the interview in the studio."

In Germany they seem to have little problems with in-studio interviewing. One reporter said: "It really doesn't matter; the Chancellor can be on the set, but it's not the normal thing." Another reported said: "It should be in the studio if it's important enough, but we don't do it often."

THE SELECTION AND IDENTITY
OF THE INTERVIEWEES

As we have seen, there is variability among the countries in the relative use of politicians, experts, random people, and the like, as interviewees. What is the rationale behind this differential selection on the part of the interviewers? In Britain I was told that "the politician often tries to get to be interviewed; the choice is always ours. The criteria are: do they have something to answer or give information we don't already have?" In the United States I was also told that "knowing the person is important, it should be someone who is articulate, who doesn't ramble, who is good on TV. It helps if people have a title—it gives instant identification." Indeed, being articulate and presentable was stressed by many of those I spoke to. Sometimes balance is important too, I was told in Israel.

What about choosing experts on various topics? In Germany the television reporters told me that they have "independent" experts, since "all experts have party affiliations, and since many experts are paid by the government they tend to protect the government." Another reporter added: "You have to read about the topic and you must know he [the expert] is responsible. In each ministry there is the person responsible. I select because of his capacity, and personal contacts, sometimes. Sometimes you have to go to the opposition too."

In Britain I was told by one reporter: "We have lists of contacts whom we can trust. They need to be visually, academically and intellectually all right, and they need to speak good language." Another reported added: "There's a lot of luck in this; on the phone he might sound great, but when you turn on the camera he might go to pieces." Indeed, the ability of the experts to speak well was stressed by most of the reporters.

In Israel I was told that the expert must be selected on the basis of what he knows and also based on his appearance and his ability to be articulate. It was also stressed, however, that "the expert cannot be used over and over again because he becomes too familiar with the audience."

And in one of the U.S. networks, I was told, "The most important thing is knowing the people. You want someone who is articulate, who doesn't ramble, who is good on TV. It helps if people have a title, it gives instant identification. You don't have to use a super [a printed caption with the person's name at the bottom of the screen] if you've identified him, but you must identify the person."

Finally, I asked about the use of the man in the street (or *vox pop*) interview. Here I got quite mixed reactions. One of the U.S. reporters snapped: "It's an exercise in futility! It doesn't contribute to knowledge, you're obliged to balance opinions, so on 'Star Wars,' for example, you end up with one who says yes and the other says no, so what are you going to tell the American people?" Another person on the same network told me something quite to the contrary: "It's fun when it's done, sometimes it even works. That's part of the entertainment element of the news. It's a valid journalistic device. It's not scientific, but you get a feel or flavor of what people think."

In Germany, once again, we got varied opinions. One reporter said: "We don't do it often; we have public opinion polling which is exact, but not the man-in-the-street! It's dangerous!" On the other hand, one of this reporter's colleagues disagrees: "We should do the interview and simply use people who are able to speak German. In editing I would use answers that say something. I would go for balance but not on demographic characteristics of the speakers."

In Israel one reporter suggests, "I would choose the people according to what they have to say and what they look like. I wouldn't approach just anybody. I don't like to use silly looking or awkward looking people." And in Britain one reporter noted, "You cannot make a reasonable judgment until you've spoken to someone so you usually just take many shots of people. You don't necessarily look for balance, because you might easily get a false balance, with one giving one side of the story and the other appearing to give the other side. That's not true balance."

THE USE OF THE MICROPHONE

It will be recalled that we found a large degree of variation in the kind of microphone used by the reporters in the four countries, with Germany in particular leading in the use of the hand-held mike. I asked the reporters about the way they prefer to use the microphone.

Generally, the German reporters are aware of the fact that they use the hand-held mike frequently. However, when I inquired why this is so I often got a puzzled look. One reporter said: "I really don't know why. Most of the time I am as nervous as the man I need to interview, so it's nice to have something in your hand." I then suggested the possibility that they prefer this kind of microphone in order to gain better control of the interviewee, and one reporter said: "Control? You are the first one to give me this idea, but it is possible." This reporter's colleague added: "It could be a means of control but I don't find it useful."

In Israel, where reporters also use the hand-held microphone relatively often, the reporters told me that they don't like it, since it involves a technical chore with which they don't want to bother, but they often have no choice since it is the easiest to set up on location.

In Britain I got a different impression. One veteran reporter was only concerned with the quality of the sound being picked up, and felt that when a stick (hand-held) mike was needed that would be all right. However, three other reporters still indicated opposition to the hand-held mike. One said, "The hand mike gives you something else to think about and it makes you look as if you're taking charge, and that doesn't help." The second added, "I want a mike I don't need to handle. For control? No! A hand mike distracts the participants and the viewers." The third reporter reiterated: "The hand one gets in the way; it doesn't look neat; you don't need the mike for control."

Finally, the U.S. reporters pushed the issue even further. As one reporter said: "A hand mike is an encumbrance; when you talk to someone it is a physical barrier and you want to break down barriers; it is intrusive and rude." Another reporter said, "The more artificiality you can remove, the better! I hate hand mikes. It's amateurish! It's unbelievably difficult to talk and move your hand at the same time. The U.S. networks would not do that—maybe some Europeans would, not Americans. That is a much lower standard!" When asked about the possibility of using the hand mike for control, one reporter even suggested a possible boomerang effect: "When you put the microphone in someone's face, he might try and grab it."

THE ANSWER IS . . . WHAT WAS THE QUESTION?

The next point I raised has to do with a common phenomenon in most of the television news interviews, namely, the fact that the questions put by the reporters to the interviewees are not heard by the audience. I asked the reporters what they felt about this and how they thought it might affect the credibility of the interview. My assumption was that in presenting the question with the answer there is less of a chance that the reporter could be accused by viewers (or by the interviewee) of taking the answer out of the context in which it was given. In their responses to these questions it was clearly evident that the interviewers were aware that this was a delicate point, hence there were some apologetic reactions and first references to the ability of the audience to deal with the information. Here, too, as with many of the other issues, there were gradations in the responses across the countries.

The West German reporters by and large believed that the questions should be heard. As one reporter put it, "The questions should be heard. When it's not heard they've done something wrong!" Another reporter agreed, adding, "But sometimes, between the question and the answer there are some irrelevant phrases, so it is all taken out." The third German reporter stated that "in any event, the first question asked must be heard; it helps the credibility."

A diametrically opposed position was suggested by one of the British reporters: "The first question—almost never! The next, if there is one, probably, if the package requires this. The first question is given to the news reader to read." What we see here, then, is a difference in style, that is, the first question should appear, but not necessarily by the reporter, but by the anchor. Another reporter stated this somewhat differently: "It will always appear in some form, it has to be contained in the package in some way. It may be paraphrased but it's got to be there. Otherwise it's meaningless." And still another newsperson said: "It looks nicer and slicker if the answers flow from the text, but you must make sure that you don't misinterpret what was said when making up the text."

The position expressed by the Israeli newsperson was somewhat ambivalent. One reported noted, "Leaving the question in serves an important purpose, but it can be taken out if it doesn't disturb the piece. It can be edited out as long as you do justice to the contents and to the veracity of what is being said."

The U.S. reporters expressed basically a similar viewpoint, but went even further in stressing the format of the television news package, on the one hand and their perception of the audience on the other hand. As one reported argued, "No problem! It's a production value! You need to lead in correctly. You must set the audience up so they have the question in their mind, so they know the question. The dialogue is not important because this is not a conversation—at the most there are two questions. We're presuming that the answer is not taken out of context." Another reporter said, "I don't think the audience cares much, but you have to be careful you don't construct a lead-in to an answer that is not reflective of the intent of the question. The question is almost always less important than the answer!" Finally, a slightly different view was expressed by another reporter: "Our style of editing is faster. Viewers are sophisticated, they know there was a question! That's what trust is all about! If I ever took a wrong answer to a question, somebody should and would expose that, and there goes all your reputation."

ASKING THE QUESTIONS

A point that has been stressed time and again is the fact that the essence of an interview is the questions asked and the answers given. In the cross-cultural context we have noticed significant differences on various points concerning the way the questions are used and formulated. Naturally this became one of the focal points of my interviews with the reporters.

The first aspect related to the use of the questions in the interview was the way the reporters prepare for the interview. I examined this from two perspectives: the actual preparation of the questions on the part of the interviewer and the extent to which the reporter prepared his interviewee by telling him in advance about what he was going to ask. It should be noted that this kind of information is only obtainable from such conversations with reporters, since by looking at the interviews as they appear on the screen we cannot determine if and how the interview was prepared (except, of course, to comment when it seems that the interview was not properly prepared given the way it was conducted).

I asked the reporters directly whether or not they prepare for the interview, and particularly if they plan ahead of time what questions they are going to ask. In all four countries I got essentially the same replies—"It depends!" The main distinction drawn was between interviews with people concerning unplanned events, in which case, as a British reporter said, "I plan as much time as it takes me to get there," and interviews scheduled ahead of time, which prompted the following comment, also from a British reporter: "If it's for a major interview, like with the Prime Minister, much preparation because nobody is better in picking up the ignorance of the reporter than the P.M." As far as the actual amount of preparation is concerned, one U.S. reporter summed it up this way: "It depends, maybe a few seconds, maybe 30-45 minutes, maybe ten years!"

As for the way in which reporters brief and prepare their prospective interviewees, here, once again, we do find intercountry variability. Once again the West German reporters reveal a relatively interviewee-oriented position. By this I mean that they are generally more willing to provide the interviewee with advanced information on the nature and intent of the forthcoming interview, but they do this with reservation. As one reporter noted: "Some want to know, some don't! We give the general line but not the exact questions." However, one of this reporter's colleagues slightly disagreed with his assessment: "From time to time we do give the questions because he [the interviewee] must be very short, he must concentrate, and therefore I talk about it. Sometimes he is given a chance to prepare."

In Britain the typical response to this question was that the general line of the intended questions is usually given to the interviewee, but not the specific questions. A distinction was drawn by one of the reporters between the live and prerecorded interview: "In the live interview there will be a brief discussion before its starts on the general area but specific questions will rarely be given." There are exceptions to the rule, however, as this British newsperson reported: "Kadaffi, for example, has agreed to give interviews only if he gets the questions ahead of time. Sometimes we have no choice if we want the interview."

The Israeli reporters distinguish between two kind of interviewing situations. If the reporter is an expert, particularly an academician, who needs to prepare information for the interview, "then by all means"; but if he is a partner who must defend himself, then "Heaven forbid! If you ask him at three P.M. why he fired so and so, he may reinstate him by the time we come down to do the interview before air time."

It seems that with regard to the issue of providing the questions ahead of time, the U.S. reporters had some interesting qualifications. One reporter, for example, said, "Almost never, but when a person is terribly nervous I will tell the area. For a head of state you sometimes need to screen the questions, but you make that clear to your audience. We have all compromised in certain ways but I wouldn't do it without the audience knowing. I would not pretend it was a free wheeling interview if I was told I could not ask certain questions." One of the reporters, who has interviewed many non-U.S. interviewees, commented, "The only courtesy would be to people for whom English is a second language. You'll tell him the area of the questions, only because of the language. They say they want to be sure they understand the questions and that their answer is understood." Finally, one reported quipped, "Sometimes I tell them the general field, I never reveal the questions, though; I honestly don't even know them . . . "

REPEATING AND INTERRUPTING

During the course of the interview, the interviewer might wish to repeat a question or interrupt the interviewee either if the response to the question is not given at all or if the response is not considered as an adequate reply. Some of this "strategy" of questioning is seen on the screen, but usually it is edited out, as we have noted in the relative infrequency of these phenomena. However, in order to find out more about what happens "behind the scenes" of the interview, I asked the reporters whether or not they feel comfortable with the interviewee and actually repeat the same question and interrupted him or her.

In Germany one of the reporters said, concerning the repetition of questions: "You can ask as often as you want, he'll say what he wants to. If he says that he only wants to answer this way, you can't force him to answer." As for interrupting the interviewee, a typical comment was as follows: "Seldom, because we only have two minutes; besides, they generally talk to the point." When I pressed a bit further I was told at length: "The English language is better because it is less complicated. It also has a better tradition of democracy in political journalism than we have. We still suffer from the authoritarian background. If I put a very hard question to whoever it is, I get very angry letters from people who say 'that's not the way to treat the minister' or 'how dare you?' English is easier because you can ask very short questions. Germans in general tend to be very complete and perfect in everything so you put the whole problem into one question, and coupled with the complex grammar it becomes very unelegant. And we are told that we must be very respectful towards the minister."

In Israel the reaction was: "You can repeat the question until you are convinced that you will not get an answer. If you feel that the person is lying or evading the issue, you may politely pursue your mission." Another reporter said, "Repeating is fine as long as I think I'll get a reply. After two attempts, go on to the next point." As for interrupting the speaker, I was told about the so-called 'In the beginning' syndrome." According to this reporter, the Israeli interviewee tends to filibuster and to explain at great length something that could be told very succinctly. "When I ask, for example, 'why did you fire so and so?' I usually get a response 'well, when I took office, I took upon myself . . . '—well, there goes a whole minute already!"

The general feeling among the British reporters is that it is all right to repeat questions, but it should be done tactfully. For example: "Thank you Prime Minister, but what I actually asked was . . . " Another reporter added, "The trouble with this is that you don't have enough time. If the guy insists on not answering after you asked twice, you just have to carry on. You have to do it enough, however, so that the viewer is aware that the person doesn't want to answer the question. Then you can go on to something else." As for interruptions, however, here I sensed more reluctance on the part of the British reporters: "It's very difficult, you must rely on instinct." Another said, "Sometimes, but I would do it nonverbally. You don't want to do it in the audio because you can ruin the whole answer." And finally, a third way of putting this is as follows: "I can never remember cutting off in mid-sentence. The interviewer would use his best diplomatic politesse to say something like 'I'm afraid we must leave it here.' He would also interject 'I think we've covered this point, let's please go to another thing.' When not speaking to the point, a good interviewer would be flexible and the bad interviewer would go on with his or her plan despite an interesting development."

As for the U.S. interviewers, it seems that here we have the most categorical attitude. On repeating the questions, one reporter said, "Hundreds of times! As long as it takes to get the answer. If the person repeatedly refuses to answer the question I would use that. But I don't believe in grand-standing. If I can explain something even if it took longer, I'd rather explain it clearly than just have good TV." Another reporter said: "As often as possible until you feel you are being rude. If the guy has really come to an end as far as what he wants to say, that's where the interview should come to an end. I would use the unwillingness to respond in the story, but then only with politicians." As far as interruptions are concerned, one reporter said, "Sure, if he's not answering question's or making a political speech." Another simply said, "No problem with that!" And a third reporter agreed, "Oh, yes, you need to be polite at first, but if I initiate the interview the agenda is mine and I got to ask the questions."

WHAT?! . . . ME?! . . . NEVER!

Part of the rapport and the aura of credibility might be established, or possibly hindered, if the reporter approaches the interviewee by his or her first name, and vice versa, that is, if the interviewee refers to the reporter by his or her first name. I asked about this question of interpersonal reciprocity.

Among the U.S. reporters I found the least objection, although there were also exceptions. One of the U.S. reporters said, "I'd rather not! In the familiarity of TV in America I'm often called Tom by people I've never met before. A newly elected prime minister of an Asian country did so in an interview with me recently. I left it in because it didn't seem to be terribly important one way or another, but I'd rather they didn't. It cuts both ways—sometimes you are flattered that they feel they know you and sometimes they genuinely do know you. Sometimes people try to rub off against your credibility by showing some intimacy that is simply not there." Another reporter said: "Never! It's not Tom, Dan or Peter out there, it's the correspondent, and whoever the other person is, it is someone of some consequence. We are more informal than the British, and I know that some Americans do use first names." Finally, a dilemma was expressed by another reporter: "It varies! I don't have a formal position. I do what I think seems right. If I do an interview for air, I tend to be formal. If I know I'll only take a [sound] bite, and I know the person, I'd call the person by their first name. The more political they are, the more they use your first name in every sentence—'well, Jim, that's an interesting question' or 'you know, Jim, I didn't want to answer that but I will.' I generally cut it off; it's obsequious, and it's self serving, silly." Another reporter, without being asked to do so, made a comparison on this point with the British reporters: "I do whatever is natural. The British are very pompous, extremely conscious of their position. British journalists are conscious of their role in society and their class stature. In America the first name approach raises the correspondent to a higher level, an indication that they are known."

What do the British reporters say about this topic? One reaction: "Not on camera! Wouldn't dream of it. We might do it by accident, and if possible I would then like to re-record that part of the interview. I don't want it to look cosy." Another reporter said, "I would never do that! It could slip but it destroys the distance that an interviewer should have from an interviewee. They come right back with the surname—'And I will tell you Mr. so and so' because I have just said to him 'Come on, Mr. Scargill . . . ' He wants to create balance, almost like an orchestrated concert. Most would not use my first name, and I wouldn't want them to do so. I don't recall it ever having happened, but I think I would try to edit it out, if possible." Another comment: "A child or a pop star, OK; but a politician, never! The respondent occasionally does, it's quite sly, generally by politicians. It sounds patronizing. Americans do it all the time and to them it is a gesture of friendship." And finally, another British reporter: "Not on the screen. I don't use the answer if it happens. It implies an over-familiarity between the interviewer and the respondent. It destroys the objectivity. People will think you are buddies. But Americans use it!"

The Israeli position seems closer to the one expressed in the United States. One reporter said, "I would not use a politician's first name, and I would try to avoid the first name of the man in the street, but it really doesn't bother me. I wouldn't edit it out." Another reporter told me: "I rarely use it, only when it is justified. I would definitely call another reporter by his first name, but not a cabinet minister. When he does so to me, I disregard it. It doesn't trouble me unless he tries to control me. Whenever national leaders become angry at us reporters, I feel good! If I had to choose, I would go for the American approach more than that of the British."

Finally, in Germany, the position can be expressed in very unequivocal terms. As one reporter put it: "What?! Me?! Never!!!" When I suggested to him that it is done sometimes, he retorted: "Yes? Where???" This feeling was unreservedly shared by all the reporters I spoke to in Germany.

COME IN REAL CLOSE . . .

I discussed with the reporters the questions of what kind of picture frame should be used in the interview, and particularly how close the frame of the interviewee should be. I pointed out the fact that an extreme close-up, from the forehead to the chin, is a shot that is unnatural in the sense that nobody can see another person from so close and still have the frame in focus unless one uses video (or film). I also asked the reporters who makes the decision as to what visual frame to shoot.

The latter question is easy to discuss, simply because there was near total consensus among the reporters in the four countries that the decision on which frame to use is left up to the cameraperson. On rare occasions, I was told, does the reporter intervene in this decision, and then always in consultation with the cameraperson. As one reporter put it: "I cannot tell the cameraman what to do. He is responsible for the picture just as I am responsible for asking the question. It is team work!" By and large all the reporters seemed to share this opinion.

However, as far as the use of various picture frames is concerned, here, once again, I got varying opinions which were highly consistent within each country and formed a continuum with substantial differences from country to country. I shall begin with the position expressed by the British reporters as they take a relatively extreme position on the one hand. "Not chin to forehead, only from the tie" said one British reporter, and proceeded: "Too close looks aggressive, it's not fair! It looks like you're interrogating the person. It's unprofessional!" Another reporter went even further: "If the person breaks down the cameraman would probably pull out, not go in. I'd never tell the cameraman to come in, we're not here to editorialize. If you're accusing a man of lying, you should tell him so, not by visual manipulation, especially since he's not aware at the time it's done what the camera is showing." Still another comment included: "Usually, head and shoulders. No closer or it distorts, no further away or he ceases to be important. Too close discloses too many imperfections in peoples' faces. I want the camera to see what I normally see when I'm talking to you, which is your head and shoulders, 5-6 feet away." Finally, a British reporter said: "They [cameramen] are aware of the effect of an intrusive or a bad taste picture would have on the public. Can't remember this kind of case."

According to the West Germans, the visual process is as follows: "I place the question and we are both in the picture. When the answer begins he [cameraman] brings the interviewee in. We come to a medium shot." As for close-up shots: "We are told not to do them. We should go from the tie, we need space for the name and title." Another reporter added: "If you feel the answer is not truthful then we must concentrate on the face. Mostly they tell the truth, in a certain way, but they don't tell the whole truth. If someone is nervous, a close-up is OK." A third reporter said: "As close as possible, but not an extreme close-up, normally from the tie, very rarely to extreme close-up. You will never find an extreme close-up of a German cabinet minister. It is considered offensive."

THE REPORTER ON CAMERA: NECESSITY OR CELEBRITY?

The major focus in the television news interviews is, of course, on the interviewee. However, sometimes the interviewer-reporter is also seen on camera. This can occur in several different ways: in an establishing shot, in which case both parties can be seen or the interviewee is seen from behind the interviewer's shoulder; in a cut-away (or "reaction") shot, which is used in order to join via editing two segments of the interview (in which case the reporter is often only seen nodding his or her head); and in a situation in which the reporter is actually seen, alone or together with the interviewee, while asking a question. Do these variations have any particular meaning in the interviewing context? Particularly, is it important for the reporter to be seen? I asked the reporters about this.

The position expressed by the British reporters is clearly that the "reaction shot" is only a technical device, used only for editing, and that "the reaction of the interviewer is really not all that relevant." Moreover, there seems to be a consensus of feeling that the notion of celebrity is not pertinent to news interviewing, and that the presence or absence of the reporter on the screen does not seem to make a difference.

The German position as expressed by the reporters I spoke to was similar to that of the British. The reaction shot is used, they suggest, mainly as an editing technique, since "the reporter is not the most important person." Nonetheless, I got the impression that the use of the reaction shot would not be ruled out if possible, as one reporter indicated: "For this we need two cameras, and we only use one." However, another German reporter added in this connection: "It depends on the number of cameras, and we use two cameras on location, also." As for the celebrity question, it seems that the Germans were more aware of this point, as compared with the British, or at least they were more willing to admit it. As one reporter said: "If you do the job long enough people think you are a celebrity." Another admitted: "It depends. Some like to be in front of the camera. In America the reporters are more interested in being in front of the camera."

The Israeli position on the issue is even more straightforward. As one reporter put it: "The way it is done now it is merely a technical thing, but if we had two cameras it would be much better." His colleague, who also serves as a news anchor, stated his point in a more direct manner: "What is this all about? One asks a question and the other answers, what could be more natural? To some extent the news is a show, and people are not robots. Both should be seen as much as possible." As for the celebrity notion, this reporter indicated: "There is a myth about interviewing, including people like David Frost and Robin Day. Most interviewing is more standard. In any event there is an element of being a celebrity. The public is afraid of a person who is considered to be an 'interrogator,' although I think this is somewhat dissipating these days as the media are becoming a bit worried of their own power."

In the United States several reporters noted an even clearer distinction between the way a regular reporter and an anchorperson appear during the course of an interview. One reporter said: "They [reaction shots] are wrong! Why cut away from the face of the interviewee? I don't do reverse shots either. They don't look right! They aren't ethical either!" Another reporter talked about the credibility of the situation: "There are times you want to show that the reporter was there so you take the two-shot over the reporter's shoulder." As for being celebrities, there seems to be little disagreement on this, although the reporters I talked to tended to hint that it happens more with their colleagues, not with themselves. As one reporter noted, "Sure! But I won't give examples. Some reporters cover themselves instead of the stories!" Another said, "It happens all the time. There are people who go into it with that in mind. There's a lot of grand-standing in this business, and it's very unfortunate." Finally, a veteran reporter said, "In my case, zero, but in the case of my anchor 99% or 100%! American TV thinks its news is enhanced by creating personalities. Why does X [my omission] coming to Y [ditto] to do a special segment report have all the extra weight if I know the place anyway and I'm there? Answer: because I don't carry enough weight with the audience but X does!"

CONCLUSION

It seems that this chapter has clearly revealed that significant and meaningful differences exist among the way reporters in the four countries treat and relate to television news interviewing. As a matter of fact, from time to time in the course of this chapter I have given examples of reporters who compared their own system with that of their competition within their own country or even with television news in other countries. I had not asked them to do so, however, until the end of my interviews with them. It is interesting, I believe, that they, too, felt the need to compare their news to other news in making their judgments. In any event, I begin the next chapter with a summary of what the reporters had to say about interviewing elsewhere, and I later make an attempt to put these differences in a more general social, cultural, and media context, thereby reconciling some of the seemingly contradictory findings in this volume.

7

RECONCILING THE DIFFERENCES: A CULTURAL INTERPRETATION

While the general format of TV newscasts in Western countries is quite similar, due to shared professional norms and values, the interviewing done in the news is different. An attempt is made to explain the differences by means of social, cultural, and political factors in the various countries.

In the last four chapters I have sought to give three different perspectives on the television news interview: what the academic and professional literature says about it; what some empirical content analytical data show; and what reporters who actually engage in such interviewing think about the phenomenon. It should be clear by now that in some respects there is agreement among these three sources of information; in others, however, there is considerable disagreement, particularly as far as the intercountry picture is concerned. This chapter is devoted to trying to understand the differences found, both among the three information sources and among the four countries studied. In doing so I shall attempt to frame the discussion into a wider social and cultural context, taking into account some aspects that can distinguish among the different societies as well as the media structure in the various countries.

Toward the end of the interview sessions that I conducted with the reporters in the four countries, I asked them to compare and contrast the way television news interviews are conducted in their own country (and network) with that of the other countries and the other networks in their country (except for Israel where there is only one network). I also asked the reporters in the United States to consider the differences between national network news and local news in the United States as another level of comparison (this was not done in the other three countries since the production of local news there, when it exists at all, is much less elaborate than in the United States).

Let us begin the interpretation segment of the findings by citing some of the comments that the reporters had to say in comparing the different news systems. This input is very revealing since it points to those specific elements that the news people themselves feel are done well or could be improved. I must point out, however, that some of the reporters I spoke to felt they were not familiar enough with the news in other countries so the excerpts are not based on all the reporters.

THE GERMAN VIEW

Let us begin with the West German journalists. Two aspects of the interviewing process seem to come up in particular: the language of interviewing and respect toward the interviewee. One reporter put it this way: "People here say 'Look to the British and American interviews! They are tough and hard, they are to the point!' I don't think they are so much better than we are, but they have the language on their side. English is a good interviewing language. Questions can be short while German is a difficult interviewing language."

Indeed, the language point came up with the German reporters and was already mentioned in the previous chapter. The typical German sentence is long and complex, it takes precious broadcast time to have the whole question heard, but then this is what the German tradition would require in "being very complete and perfect in everything." One way to overcome this problem was developed by German television newspeople, namely, using what they call "key words." These are terms reporters use as stimuli in order to get the interviewee (mainly politicians—as so many of German interviewees are indeed politicians) to begin talking about a particular topic. Using the "key word" alleviates the need to preface the topic with a long exposition and explanation. The "key words" rapidly become associated with a particular issue in the news, and even the audience picks them up and presumably understands them. Thus, for example, the reporter might say: "What about 'terror'?" and the interviewee will know exactly what is being referred to.

Incidentally, the news anchor on the German television literally "reads" the news, holding a set of papers in his or her hand, and rarely lifts his or her eyes directly at the camera. In other German television programs in which a "host" or "master of ceremonies" faces the camera, the teleprompter is used. However, it is not used on the news. I asked about this and was told that reading the news must appear official, correct, and precise. Thus reading from paper is indicative of this precision. Moreover, I was told that the two West German television networks have a pool of anchorpeople who read the news, and that they do not subscribe to the American way, whereby the anchor becomes a star. The reason for this, as described to me, was that they wish to avoid the extreme level of personification that characterizes American news. They do not want the viewer to face a "star" who knows everything, who is the official person presenting the news, and with whom they can identify, and even "worship" at times. I was even told by one West German television official that this notion was one of the lessons of twentieth century history in Germany.

As for the respect paid by German reporters to their interviewees, here is what I was told: "I have seen U.S. news. We should have more such interviews. They interrupt him, it's not such a friendly way. We have a system of asking the person which question he wants to be asked. You are in danger of doing this. American politicians must answer the questions otherwise the journalist is not so polite like the German journalist. It is a cultural difference—the Americans are tougher, they come to the point; yes, it's culturally different. Sometimes our situation is comparable, however, but not often. It's only in America!" Another German reported added: "German interviews have more visible respect. Not as tough, and should be tougher. Should use the revolver technique—Bang! Bang! Bang!"

This image that German reporters have of the U.S. news and its interviewers is interesting. It is indeed clear, as the data presented in Chapter 5 has indicated, that German television interviewing can be characterized as very formal. This is the case with respect to the topics in the news that contain interviews, whereby more than half of the interviews are in items on internal politics, and hardly any interviewing at all is present in "human interest" news items (which don't appear frequently in the news anyway). This is even more pronounced in the extremely high percentage of "public official" interviewees, more than in any of the other countries examined. Thus there is no question about the fact that German television news is official in nature.

Moreover, when we look at the "complaints" of the German reporters, and their "fantasizing" about being tough interviewers, the data I have presented portrays them in a relatively mild position. Although they interrupted more than the U.S. and British reporters (in as many as 6% of the interviews) they asked relatively fewer provocative questions and they did not repeat their questions on the air very frequently. And we must not forget their deep aversion at the thought of using the first name of the interviewees.

As for the differences between the two German networks, ARD and ZDF, according to the reporters from both networks that I spoke to there are no significant differences, although the reporters would have liked to see some. As one reporter put it: "In general, we are the same.

Should it be the same? I think there should be differences but there are not enough ways." It should be recalled that each of the two German networks is identified by public opinion as being somewhat affiliated with one of the major political parties in Germany (note the numerous references of the reporters to politicians and the overrepresentation of politics and politicians in the German news). In any event, this does have some bearing on the way the two networks conduct their respective news operation. The ZDF is perceived to be more closely associated with the Christian Democratic Party (CDU), whereas the ARD is seen to be tied more closely to the Social Democrats (SPD), although perhaps in a weaker way. Accordingly, the ARD news is a bit more formal, whereas the ZDF may be considered as a bit lighter. It should be noted, however, that the sample used in this study of news interviewing was too small to detect any differences between the two networks.

THE BRITISH VIEW

There seems to be little consensus between the BBC correspondents and the ITN correspondents concerning the two networks and the nature of the news product they both produce. There was much agreement within each network, however. Thus one of the BBC reporters told me, "We are very much the same, we use the same techniques. There can't be that much difference. News is a record of what happened and interviewing is one technique. It's got to be short and sharp." This reporter's colleague added, "Oh, yes, we're similar; we're just trying to do the same job!" At the ITN, however, the position was quite different: "Their [the BBC] philosophy is the same as ours and the intentions should be the same. But, we are better in selecting, questioning, etc. We are more probing, but not aggressive." This reporter added, "We are more incisive than colleagues at the BBC. It's really the hungry against the over-fed, in a word."

When I asked the British reporters about their view of news interviewing in the other countries of the study, their focus went primarily on the United States. Moreover, on this level, there was agreement between the two British networks. As one reporter put it: "In America it's far more aggressive; in continental Europe it's less probing. We're probably in-between the two. You've got to remember British sensibilities. We like to try to interview with the velvet glove. We don't want to be seen as aggressive; we want to be probing; we want to do it courteously and be seen to do it courteously. I don't say the Americans do not interview courteously; I think they will sometimes go further than we will. The American would claim that a British network of journalists would never have discovered a Watergate. Now that's highly arguable, but there is something in that."

Another reporter told me: "I wouldn't say our way is like the American. I think they have a lot to learn from us, like letting things run rather than making God of brevity. They spend vast amounts of money to send correspondents to various parts of the world and they don't use them. If we spent money on that, we'll use what they send back to the best of our ability." Brevity came up again by other reporters: "Theirs [American] are shorter. Their inflections are wrong. Three to four seconds is very short. Before you can look up and see who he is, he's gone! It inhibits rather than encourages understanding." And finally, another reporter went even further: "I hate the Americans' tightly edited pieces when they don't let pictures run and they use eight seconds of an interview. To me, whether my brain is slower than other people, it gives you no time to absorb what that person is trying to say. I think it's some rule that each correspondent has a minute and they've got to get everything into that minute. It's terrible! Some of my colleagues like it but I hate it! There's a great temptation to be slick and fast, but it's terrible!" So much for that.

THE ISRAELI VIEW

The Israeli news, which is presented on the country's only station, contains relatively many news items from abroad, some of which come from the news correspondents of Israel Television who are stationed in a few of the world's major capitals (although there has been a decrease in recent years due to budget cuts), and others are purchased from the European Broadcasting Union (EBU), which provides a news exchange for its member countries. Thus Israeli reporters and the Israeli viewing public are quite familiar with the way news is presented in other countries. This, I would suggest, is quite different from the other countries in this study, mainly the United States, which relies almost entirely on its own U.S. correspondents and hardly ever purchases news items from other countries. The German and British television networks are also active members of the EBU, and they, too, tend to use items obtained through the news exchange.

Given the relatively high familiarity with foreign news reporting, the Israeli reporters were quite able to suggest a "model" concerning the position of Israeli television news within the context of the other countries. One reporter told me: "We are closer to the British-German model, less to that of the United States. We prefer the European model, and if we ever get to the level of the BBC, it would be great!" Another reporter was more specific: "I am not impressed by the German news—it is quite boring. As for England, they have a speaking and broadcast culture which we should learn from, including what they do in interviewing. They are more professional. So are the Americans."

THE AMERICAN VIEW

Not all of the U.S. reporters seemed comfortable with drawing comparisons between their own networks and television news interviewing in other countries, perhaps due to lack of familiarity with how it is done overseas. Those who did speak on the issue had some criticism, particularly of the German and the British news. One reporter said: "I feel they [the British] have more time and I'm envious of them. We are so packaged and scheduled and there's such a formula, it would be nice if we had time to do other things." Another reporter put is this way: "The news is part of the whole show business syndrome; it's vital and there's no getting away from it! It must not be gratuitous drama, rather it must make a point." The show business element came up in another reporter's comments: "I lived in Germany. Germans are heavy-handed. They don't pay attention to production values. Let's say a good word about production values! There's every reason why it should not be dull, long, uninteresting. It should go smoothly. The Germans, as meticulous as they are, are not very meticulous in their program and a lot of it tends to be very very dull. Their product is not as slick as ours. None of them go for the star system. The powers that be [in the United States] have decided that the star system works. Uncle Walter was someone people believed in. There is a good reason why a person should do the news every day. Germans don't do it. The BBC, too, makes a fetish about non-identification."

Asked about the differences between the networks, one reporter said: "It depends on the correspondents, not on the networks. The correspondents are interchangeable, they switch around." Another reporter agreed and put it in unequivocal terms: "Correspondents are no different! Networks are no different! There should be no difference! If you find any differences between the networks, it is pure chance. There is no overall philosophy about the news interview.

EYEWITNESSING THE ACTION:
INTERVIEWING IN U.S. LOCAL NEWS

As I have indicated earlier, among the countries I examined in this study, only in the United States are there special newscasts, indeed many of them, devoted to "local" news. Although I have not done a systematic analysis of the interviews in that format (see the profiles in Chapter 2), it seems that some manifest differences can be pointed out. For example, relatively more interviews are done live, on location, given the ability of local stations to send helicopters to the scenes of events nearby, and the more recently increased use of reports via satellite from the "Washington bureau" direct to the local station; as a result more questions are heard; more local and "man-in-the-street"-type interviewees appear; more human interest stories containing interviews seem to be shown; and the interviewer-reporter appears in a much more star-like role.

As can be expected, the national network reporters, many of whom got to where they are after being local news reporters, are generally not pleased with this situation. As one reporter put it: "Many [local] reporters will lead a person. There's been a tragedy and the questions will be: 'Would you say this is the worst tragedy that's ever happened to you in your whole life?' or 'Would you say that you don't know where you're going to go from here?' That's crap! That's show business. There are some good local news journalists, but most are out to earn the big buck and to become anchors." Another reporter added, "People exist in local news to make stars of themselves. I have nothing but terrible things to say about most local news. I think that for the most part they don't care about the news, they don't care about getting information, and they don't care about their audience—all they care about is making stars of themselves, and I find it mostly disgraceful!"

In order to illustrate some aspects of local news interviewing, I spoke to a few local reporters in Buffalo, New York, and asked them essentially the same questions as I put to the national news reporters. On most of the issues there seemed to be almost total consensus among the local newspeople I spoke to. Following are excerpts of what they had to say on some of the issues.

On general satisfaction with interviewing in the news: "Would like more length and depth. We have conflicting demands, to get more information but not to bore the viewers and turn them off. It could be tougher if the interviewer does his homework. They mostly don't get enough background."

On the reporter being a celebrity:

Ah, yes, ego gratification. You're talking about the Geraldo Rivera school of interviewing in which reversal shots are made to be dramatic. The public demands authentic interviews, people are hyped to TV, they understand the various shots. Interviews are not done with that purpose in mind, but a secondary goal is to make the interviewer look smart. It depends on how good the interviewer is, like Wallace, Donaldson and Koppel. People are interested in the technique more than in the answers. These guys go for the jugular vein. Some local people try to get sparks too.

One of the reporters gave me an example:

Last week I did a feature in which I went into a black restaurant in a black section of Buffalo. I was obviously an outsider and I interviewed people about what they had for breakfast. They talked about large biscuits and grits. Obviously I'm not a large biscuits and grits kind of guy—I don't come from the South but in one scene I had myself ordering grits, and the waitress, who was black, looked at me as if to say "you're a phony baloney." She laughed at me and I laughed at with her. It put me down, but in a sense it ingratiated me with viewers because they saw that I am a human being too. When anchors do interviewing it's to show they're working. They are also reporters, they sell their authenticity.

On interviewing in the studio: "We prefer on location where it's more authentic. On the other hand, it's nice to have the person in the studio. He's come to us and decided to talk to us in our environment. Sometimes there is an underlying message which is that we are important enough in his life that he's willing to come and talk to us."

On the preferred microphone: "The standard stick! No particular reason. You can stick a logo on it—promotion!"

On the close-up shot: "Generally the reporter decides. He knows how he wants to package the story. He might say he wants a close-up. Very close on the face is generally used in a situation where emotion is involved. When someone is crying or is very angry, it heightens the drama. It would not be considered an abnormal shot. The question is not when would you avoid an extreme close-up shot of the face, but rather when don't you do the interview. I would pick the 'better side' of a politician if it doesn't compromise the journalistic values."

On the use of the "man-in-the-street" interview: "When Vanessa Williams lost her Miss America title, it's not a really significant story in terms of the future of mankind, but everybody has an opinion and everybody is talking about it. We try to elicit popular response by talking about topics people are talking about. I don't talk to people who say they don't have an opinion on the topic. We don't make a great effort to balance, but will go by race and gender. We'd take half a dozen and show three seconds of each."

On the use of first names: "Using somebody's first name is a wonderful way to open the door of someone's egocentricity. They do use my first name and I have no feeling about it. I would expect them to use my first name. It would add to my credibility. All of us are humble and would like to be recognized. From a professional stand-point it makes no difference to me. I think it's a reflection on the culture rather than compromising on journalistic ethics."

DIFFERENT INDEED!

What we have seen, then, is that there are indeed differences between the way television news interviews are conducted and presented in the various countries we have examined. This has been exemplified both in the empirical data based on the content analysis of the interviews, as presented on the screen, and it has also been confirmed in the words of the television journalists who do the actual interviewing.

Interestingly, and surely not unexpectedly, there are differences between the two sets of data (the content analytical and the semistructured interviews with the reporters). This poses a rather curious dilemma, namely, which set of findings should we rely on and consider more trustworthy or, put more crudely, should we simply disregard one set of the findings in favor of the other? There is surely no simple answer. I believe, however, that first of all, we should reject the notion of discarding any set of findings. We must remember that the content analytical data based on 820 interviews, a rather sizable number indeed, is but a small fraction of the many interviews that are conducted in television news. Our problem is further compounded by the fact that some of the variables we were looking at, such as interruptions, role switching, and so forth are generally quite rare, and even in a sample of adequate size, as in the present case, a few cases here and there can distort the picture significantly. Thus my tentative reply to this question is to consider the content analytic findings for what they clearly demonstrate, but to use the "interpretation" offered by the reporters as a meaningful supplement to our understanding of the findings. This is despite the possibility that the reporters, in their attempt to describe the issues as they see them, are also no doubt biased due to their personal and idiosyncratic points of view.

Nonetheless, it seems that the television news interview, although usually quite brief in each single instance, is a remarkable and revealing

illustration of several central aspects of culture and society, even beyond
the narrower domain of the television culture. If we could imagine a set
of concentric circles, the inner most of which is the "news interview,"
surrounded in turn by "TV news," by "television," by "the media," and
finally by "culture" or "society"—we may be correct in suggesting that
the television news interview encapsulates some elements of its surrounding circles, which include political norms, social relationships,
aesthetic values, and rules of etiquette, just to mention a few.

Furthermore, if we examine television news in the Western world in
an overall fashion we will tend to find that most newscasts are quite
similar in their general structure, in the kind of topics that get into the
news, and in the way news items are constructed. As a matter of fact,
most Western European countries, the U.S. networks, and some middle
eastern countries actually share news items within the European
Broadcasting Union's News Exchange Service. This is the case since
journalists in Western countries share several basic news values relating
to editing and composition of news: what is considered newsworthy; the
need to present varying points of view; and objectivity (whatever that
may mean and however it can be achieved). Thus studying these
journalistic norms and values cross culturally may not yield significant
differences. The news interview, however, which appears as an important segment in numerous news items, and which involves elements of
selection and composition as well as human relations, technology,
language, and image, can exemplify whatever differences may exist in
the various cultures, above and beyond the commonly shared aspects of
the news.

The claim made by the Israeli reporters, cited earlier, that they are
more similar to the British and German model than to the U.S. model,
raises two interesting and related questions: First of all, is there such an
entity as a "model" of television news interviewing such that one can
speak of a British or German model that is different from, say, the
American model; and second, are the Israelis indeed closer to the
European model, that is, can such things be measured using any
reasonable yardstick? It seems that one can speak of some basic trends in
television news interviewing that distinguish the countries from one
another; however, it is not always the case that the British and German
form one model and that the American forms another. Rather, it seems
closer to the truth to suggest that the various countries differ from each
other on certain characteristics of the television news interview, but that
these differences do not form consistent patterns whereby one can place
each country in a clear position vis-à-vis the others, and which holds for
all the characteristics. Thus, for example, as noted in Chapter 5,

interviewing in the news in Israel occurred in 28% of all the news items, which was much closer to the situation in the United States (31%) and in Britain (39%) than to that in Germany (11%). On the other hand, in terms of the length of the interview, Israeli interviews, on the average, were almost as long as their German counterparts (with means of 41 and 44 seconds, respectively) as compared to the average 13 and 26 second interviews in the United States and Britain.

Where, then, does this lead the discussion? It seems that the most appropriate way to deal with the overall findings is to attempt to explain them using national-cultural factors as well as media organization and production factors, which can permit certain generalizations but which avoid labeling and thereby "locking in" the situation in each country into so called "models." Put another way, it seems that if news producers in a given country contemplate some changes in the format of their news, including the way interviewing is done, they most likely will decide to change the emphasis on one or several particular points rather than adopt a new model. This is despite the fact that they may refer, in a manner of speaking, to the American, British, or German "model."

NATIONAL AND MEDIA CHARACTERISTICS

It is quite dangerous to speak of national characteristics. Doing so would surely be oversimplifying and overgeneralizing matters. And yet we often find ourselves referring to certain aspects of a culture or a society which we believe is common to most, if not all, of its members. Keeping this in mind let us attempt to raise some suggestions as to why the patterns of television news interviewing in the four cultures examined are indeed the way they are. On the other hand, it seems safer to propose that certain aspects of the way the media in each of the societies is organized has some effect on the way the interviews are conducted in television news. In the following pages I shall attempt to combine and discuss both the national characteristics and the media framework, which might be relevant in explaining some of the findings concerning the interviews.

West Germany

The German national culture has often been associated, at least in a stereotypical sense, with such traits as official, authoritative, dogmatic, precise, and inflexible. These characteristics lie at the roots of the main national crisis of Germany in this century. Indeed, some of these points have been substantiated in social-psychological and anthropological research; but in any event, they are perceived by many to be true.

How, then, does this affect the way German television news interviews are conducted? First of all, as I mentioned earlier, German news on television is "read" from paper, giving the newscast an aura of officialdom and precision. Indeed, the general impression one gets when viewing German television news is a serious and somber atmosphere, with most topics being solemn and at times even grave. In all my research on television news I cannot recall a single instance of a German news anchor or reporter smiling or "editorializing" a story by raising an eyebrow on camera. Interviewing in the news is relatively rare, compared to the other countries, and when it is conducted, it is mainly with people in official capacities, mostly government. The alternative to the interviewing role is the news "reader" or reporter, and they, too, are persons with official stature. As a consequence, most interviews are conducted in government buildings or other public places, and very few in private homes with private citizens, or in out-of-door locations. Very few of the interviews are conducted with women, perhaps due to the relatively low frequency of women in such positions of power in Germany.

The interviews in Germany are the longest compared with the other countries. This is probably the result of two factors: language and respect to authority. First, the German language, which consists of long words and sentences and a complex grammatical structure (for instance, with the verb coming at the end of the sentence), which simply takes more time to express the same idea as compared to what it would take in other languages). The emphasis on respect toward authority requires the use of certain polite expressions when talking with public officials, and often requires the reporter to begin and end the interview with (and not to edit out) appropriate salutations and expression of gratitude. Moreover, being precise and punctual often requires the reporter to include in the news item the presentation of the question that was put to the interviewee so that the viewer will know that the reply was not taken out of context. Indeed, there were relatively many more questions heard in the German interviewing than in any of the other countries surveyed. And yet, German reporters ask the fewest provocative questions and interrupt relatively infrequently. They also never use the first name of the interviewee. In Germany there is more explicit identification of the interviewee than in any of the other countries studied: In only 19% of the cases was there no identification at all (the lowest among the countries) and in 36% of the cases there was both spoken and printed identification of the interviewee (much more by far compared with the other countries). These latter points seem to be strong indications of the relatively official, formal, prompt, and precise nature of the presentation of interviews in German television news.

This does not mean to suggest that the German reporter does not attempt to assert himself and to apply acceptable pressure on the interviewee in order to get a reply. It must be done, however, with much tact and courtesy. Given the inability to do so in an exaggerated manner at the verbal level, it seems that perhaps this is compensated for in the nonverbal aspects of the interview. Thus, for example, we found that the German interviews had the highest frequency of close physical proximity between the interviewer and the interviewee, a situation that can be interpreted as an attempt by the reporter to "crowd in" on the interviewee. Also, and related to this, is the use of the hand microphone, which as some of the German reporters noted, can be used to control the situation. And finally, although there were relatively more "medium shots" in Germany than in any of the other countries, there were also slightly more "extreme close-up" shots of the interviewees in the German news.

The West German two-network television system is not a highly competitive one. As noted above, each of the networks is "affiliated" with one of the two major political parties, which represents another aspect of the high concentration on political matters and interviews with politicians and public officials (note, incidentally, the frequent reference of the reporters to "politicians" in the examples they gave). The networks are well equipped with the latest technology, enabling them to do remote coverage, sophisticated editing, and so on, but this is rarely done in the news. In this sense, it seems that German television news is quite conservative and conventional but respectful and correct.

Britain

In one respect I have caused injustice to the presentation of the British findings of the study. As noted earlier, while I was only able to obtain and analyze the news interviews of the BBC, I was aware of the fact that this would not be presenting a totally comprehensive picture of British television news. Therefore, in conducting my own interviews I purposely decided to speak with reporters and news producers at the BBC as well as at Independent Television News (ITN).

We must remember that historically it was the BBC which was credited with having established and maintained for many years the traditional, and what had been referred to and acknowledged among Western countries as the "standard," television news interview. In this connection, recall the widespread British literature cited in Chapter 3, and particularly the references made by U.S. authors to British interviewers such as Robin Day. For many years the BBC was the sole producer of television news in Britain. It was mandated by Parliament as a public corporation and it was expected to maintain neutrality on issues involving controversy. Generally speaking, there is widespread consensus that the two BBC channels have lived up to this expectation. There are those who take exception to this, however, notably the Glasgow University Media Group, which claims in *Bad News* (1976) that the BBC (as well as the ITN) present a biased anti-labor coverage of economic and industrial issues in Britain. By the time the two Independent Television commercial networks entered the media scene (the latest, Channel Four, only in 1983), each with its respective news programs produced by ITN, the competition for news audiences clearly intensified. And yet, one gets the feeling (which is clearly hard to prove or disprove) that the basic formal and strict rules of parity and fairness toward all political parties and interest groups has been maintained, or at least that an effort is made to preserve them.

In a general sense, it seems that the British interviews are somewhat in the middle range compared with the other countries. General statistics support this point. Thus the length of the British interviews are in between those of the U.S. networks and the Israeli and German newscasts, and the percentage of time of the newscast devoted to interviewing is also less than in Israel but more than in the United States and Germany. Indeed, "middle of the road" is probably the best characterization of the television news interviews in Britain. While British reporters do attempt to be forceful and apply pressure on their interviewees, somewhat like the Germans, they generally do so with great caution and "correctness." As Kocher (1986) states in a comparative study of the perception of the roles of West German and British journalists: "German journalism follows the traditional role or a species of political and intellectual career, which tends to place a lot of value on opinion and less on news. British journalism, in contrast, particularly sees itself in the role of transmitter of facts, a neutral reporter of current affairs."

The concern expressed by the reporters in Britain, when discussing the use of first names of interviewees, about appearing too close to and familiar with persons in official capacities, may explain the fact that in Britain we found the lowest percentage of interviews with public officials (31% of all the interviews) and with persons elected to their positions (only 22% of all interviews). Connected to this is the fact that only 1% of all the interviews took place in government buildings (the lowest among the four countries) and 14% in the studios (the highest among the countries). This may be a reflection of the British reporters' attempt to avoid naturally biased individuals and to keep to more neutral grounds, that is, their own studios, all this in order to present themselves as being reliable and objective.

It has often been suggested that among the four countries studied, there are still indications of class consciousness in Britain. Whether or not this is so is an interesting sociological issue. In any event, this hypothesis may be reflected in the claim made by the British reporters that they would actually cut out any references of familiarity made to them during the course of the interview. Also, a measure of the physical distance between the interviewer and the interviewee indicates that in Britain the two participants in the interviews stood further apart from one another than in the other countries. Finally, in this regard, we found in Britain the highest percentage of medium shots of the interviewee and the lowest percentage of close-up shots. This, too, may be a means of maintaining interpersonal distance and avoiding the intrusion into the personal space of the interviewee. Possibly related to this is the fact that in 60% of the British interviews (a higher percentage than in any of the other countries) there was no explicit identification of the interviewees, neither verbally nor by means of printed captions.

As far as the topics of the interviews are concerned, in the British news there was the highest percentage of interviews in news items concerning "internal order" (18% of all the items) and concerning "labor" (17% of all the items). This could have been a seasonal finding, yet they are also most likely to portray conflict between social-economic classes in the population, which tend to emphasize the class structure of the society. In the present analyses I did not go into the way in which interviewees from different groups in society were presented (for instance, police versus protestors or management versus labor), mainly due to the small number of cases in each of these categories. However, it should be noted, for example, that research conducted in Britain by the Glasgow University Media Group (1976), which dealt specifically with the presentation of labor news on British television, has indicated that each of the two groups received different treatment, including interview situations, with management given a far better image.

Israel

The Israeli-born person has often been nicknamed a "sabra," the fruit of the cactus—thorny on the outside and sweet inside. Almost as an antithesis to the stereotype of the reserved and rigid German, the Israeli national character consists of such traits as daring, innovative, flexible, improvising, and audacious. It has been said that the ability of the young Israeli state to overcome some of its almost insurmountable problems in the relatively few years of its national existence has been a direct result of these characteristics.

Throughout the centuries during which the Jewish people remained in exile from their homeland, they were subjugated to the authority of the local rulers. Palestine, their ancient homeland, was under foreign rule, including the most recent British mandate which ended in 1948 with the establishment of the State of Israel. No wonder, then, that in the past 40 years or so Israelis have had to learn to live with their own independence and to create their own governmental and social institutions. Jews in the Diaspora did not have much respect for their foreign ruler, and at best they would attempt to survive with as little contact with the government as possible. In their own new state they quickly found themselves in control, but it has taken many years for the average citizen to learn to respect persons in government and authority. Thus, for example, it is common to see a crowd of bystanders rallying to the defense of a person being issued a summons by a traffic policeman for crossing against a red light.

The roots of Israeli mass communication are found in the prestate days, under British occupation. The press, including newspapers and radio, were a fighting press, launching their attacks against the "foreign" ruler. This carried over to the new state, and to television, which came to the country in 1967, quite late in the history of that medium. Israel Television is still in its relatively early developing stages, although its news department can already accept credit for several major successes, both in terms of its coverage of world media events (for instance, the visit of President Sadat of Egypt in 1977 and the war in Lebanon in 1982) and in terms of raising certain issues and placing them on the public agenda, such as the recent scandals concerning the country's security services. Finally, the facilities of Israel's single television station are much to be desired. Thus, for example, the use of standard ENG equipment, although purchased several years ago, has not been implemented due to labor disputes, hence most of the news coverage of events in Israel is still done with 16mm film.

How, then, does all this affect the way interviews are conducted in the Israeli news? The first point of interest is that interviewing in the Israeli news occupies a greater percentage of the news time (22%) than in the other countries. This is possibly due to the fact that conducting interviews, especially when they are done "live" in the news studio or on location, is a relatively cheap and quick way to fill news time. Thus it is not necessary to go out to obtain film footage, to do fancy editing, and to design and produce complex visuals. Connected to this is the fact that, as noted, most recorded interviews in Israel are still done on film, and not on video, which requires larger news teams and more time to process and edit. The best solution is to find an interviewee who is willing to come to the studio and talk, talk, and talk some more (and there is no shortage of such people around).

Indeed, the longest interview in our sample was in Israel, lasting 6½ minutes. It should be noted that although only 5% of the Israeli interviews in the sample were done in the studio, they were relatively long interviews. Moreover, often on Israeli television, the news anchor, and sometimes the reporter as well, summarize for the viewers what the interviewee has said in the interview just immediately before showing it, once again taking up more time. Finally, in this regard, of all the countries examined in this study, Israel is the only one where the scheduling of the length of the newscast is relatively flexible. Thus although the program is scheduled to be 30 minutes on week nights, the program can be extended without too much difficulty. The operating procedures indicate that the news editor can go five minutes beyond the regular half hour at his discretion, and the duty station manager can approve an even longer newscast. This is done not too infrequently when events and related news judgments warrant it. This, of course, means that there might be more and longer interviews.

The number of political parties also influences the format of interviewing in the news. In the United States only two political parties are represented in Congress, there are three parties in Britain's House of Commons, and four main parties in the West German Bundestag. In Israel, however, there are roughly 15 parties represented in the Knesset. What this means is that on many political issues several members of parliament must be given an opportunity to express themselves on the issues of the day. This, of course, is in line with the notion of balance in the presentation of news, particularly since there is only one government-controlled station. Add to this the relative lack of debating and forensic skills among Israeli politicians (which in part is due to the lack of such formal training in the Israeli educational system), and the tendency of many politicians to be "in the beginning . . ." types, hence the long-winded interviews.

In addition to the appearance of political interviewees, as in all the countries, there are relatively many "victims" of various events. This could possibly be explained by the great emphasis in Israeli society on the plight and suffering of people, probably due to the commonly shared memory of the Holocaust during World War II. Also, the relatively low frequency of appearance of "experts" in Israeli television news is not due to the lack of experts and professionals, but rather to the often expressed feeling that "I don't need advice, I know it myself," which can be heard in Israel in many circles about many things.

The use of language in conversations among Israelis has been referred to as "dugri" language, which essentially means language that is "straight to the point" or "telling it like it is." This phenomenon also finds its way into the form of interviewing in the news. There is a manner of directness, some element of "chutzpah" (audacity) and "familiarity" that often reduces the distance between the interviewer and interviewee. In this connection, note the relatively high frequency of repeated questions, provocative questions, and interruptions of the interviewee found in the Israeli sample. As for the use of first names by the participants in the interviews, although only two cases were cited by an interviewer and none by interviewees, it seems that this was a slight deviation from the true Israeli norm. Moreover, note that the Israeli reporters admit that they are not overly concerned about this.

The United States

It seems that the key concept that might explain much of what we have seen in the interviews in the U.S. news is competition. Historically, the U.S. broadcast media, television included, have been the least regulated. This is part of the philosophical tradition of the free marketplace of ideas in which regulation is only necessary to make the exchange and free flow of information possible. Hence, the legal framework for the operations of the Federal Communications Commission is relatively relaxed compared with the regulatory systems and legislation in the other countries that we have examined. As a result of this situation, there are in addition to the three original commercial networks (ABC, CBS, and NBC) and the one public broadcasting network (PBS) in the United States several other television networks as well as hundreds of television stations, many affiliated with the networks, and some independent of them. This has increased the competition for audiences in recent years to enormous proportions, mainly since viewer ratings are "converted" into advertising money and corporate revenues. Incidentally, the U.S. stations are the only ones that actually interrupt the flow of news for the sake of commercials.

Television news in the United States is big business, although in a somewhat paradoxical way. The typical U.S. television channel presents more hours of news each day than in any other country. There is news in the morning, news at noon, news in the late afternoon (mainly of the local genre, sometimes as much as two hours nonstop), followed by the prestigious evening newscasts produced by the networks, and there are news "breaks" several times during the day telling the audience what is coming up and must not be missed. And to top it all off, there is the CNN, the all-news network, for those who want to tune in at any hour of the day or night to find out what is going on. And yet, the percentage of people seeing any news (estimated at about 55%) is lower than in most Western countries.

Given the backdrop of competition, what don't the networks and their affiliated stations do to attract audiences to their news "program" or "show," as it is often referred to? First of all, they advertise their news departments in newspapers and in gigantic billboards across America. Second, they develop their own commercials, which they air depicting their own news teams and anchor(s), all in an attempt to create an image of trustworthiness and credibility, part of the process of creating and maintaining celebrities and stars. And third, they announce ahead of time what will be on the news to keep the audience glued to the screens (they do this during the course of the newscast, before the commercial breaks, and they do it during the course of the day in spot announcements as well as at the end of the newscasts, when they tell us what is "coming up" in the following evening's broadcast).

As for style, the news items are brief, they are generally written in concise terms with relatively little redundancy, the film footage is usually fast paced with sophisticated editing, there is much use of visuals and graphics, and drama and action fulfill a central role. Even in the network news, which is considered as the more serious format, there are numerous human interest stories and portraits of people in the news. The time scheduling is perfect, never ending late, so that the local commercials can be inserted at the exact preplanned time across the country. The news is "packaged" to be attractive in order to sell.

How, then, does the interview exemplify all this? The overall use of interviews in the U.S. news is moderate, with 14% of the entire time devoted to interviewing, 31% of all items with at least one interview. However, in items with at least one interview, there are on average actually 2.7 interviews, and they are very short, with an average of 13 seconds per interview, with some as short as a second, that is, a word or two uttered by the interviewee. This format can only be obtained with the very precise and professional editing procedures that are employed. From a filmic point of view the news packages that contain numerous cuts of great visual complexity are almost perfect. And yet, the American reporters, as elsewhere, complain mainly of lack of time. Indeed in the case of the U.S. interviews, it is clear what they mean.

In terms of content, the U.S. newscasts have the highest percentage of human interest stories, a news category that virtually "calls for" interviews. On the other hand, we found almost no interviews concerning labor matters and relatively little on business affairs. This is probably due to the fact that business reports are usually presented in a very "business-like" manner, such as the brief stock market reports, and that labor matters are usually reported as part of local news, except when national disputes are involved. The U.S. news had the highest percentage of American interviewees (95% of all those interviewed) and the highest percentage of "randomly" selected interviewees, most likely due to the heavy use of human interest stories and the like. The most frequent location for a U.S. interview was in an office, more than doubling office-located interviews of other countries. On the other hand, there are very few interviews in the news studio, probably because such live interviews cannot be controlled time-wise.

Since interviews have the potential for drama and confrontation, and since drama is part of the game, we find that American interviews contain many more close-up shots of the interviewee (65% of all shots were of this kind). This is part of the notion of "invading" the private space of the interviewee, namely, his or her face. It allows the viewer to see clearly the tears and sweat when the respondent is under pressure. Moreover, the relatively frequent use of first names by the reporter when approaching the interviewee can be interpreted as an attempt to break down the formal barrier, just as the camera does so in a close-up shot.

Questions are rarely heard in the U.S. news, mainly due to time constraints. But when a question does appear, there are often more questions in the same interview, some quite provocative, as the following example illustrates. On January 25th, 1984, NBC's Carl Stern interviewed a man whose application for U.S. citizenship was denied by the Supreme Court because he is an admitted homosexual—a kind of psychopath, as the Court suggested.

Stern: To you it means what if you're psychopathic?

Man: Well, someone that's psychotic, unbalanced.

Stern: Crazy?

Man: Yes. Crazy.

Stern: Are you sick or crazy?

Man: I don't think so.

Stern: Are you a threat to anyone?

Man: I don't think so.

Stern: Have you ever been in trouble?

Man: Never.

Stern: Ever been arrested?

Man: Never.

In this brief exchange, which took only several seconds, six questions were asked and six replies were given and the man's face was shown in an extreme close-up. Drama at its best!

CONCLUSION

Although the theoretical rationale and stated objectives of television news interviewing are agreed upon by most of those who engage in reporting and producing the news, it seems that there are some significant differences in the way the interviews are conducted in the various countries. This chapter has attempted to show that despite the widespread and shared notions of newspeople, which are based to a large measure on common professional, ethical, and aesthetic values, the product they produce is different. It was argued that these differences are due to a large extent to social, political, and cultural varieties, which seem to influence the way interviews are done and presented, above and beyond what is common and accepted by all. In the next and final chapter, I shall discuss some of the implications of the television news interview and offer some thoughts on where things may be going.

8

ANSWERS WITHOUT QUESTIONS: THE FUTURE OF THE TELEVISION NEWS INTERVIEW

Based upon some theoretical issues and empirical cross-national differences, while at the same time acknowledging the professional constraints of conducting interviews in the news, some suggestions are offered toward an improved approach to the subject.

At the outset this book argues that the television news interview is probably the most complex form of interviewing in journalism. It is more difficult to produce since it involves more people and equipment. It requires a series of decisions on the part of the producer, the reporter, the cameraperson, the editor, and the director. It raises some difficult potential and real problems in terms of the relationship between the journalist and the interviewees. Thus it is indeed quite remarkable that a segment of the news that often lasts only one to several seconds requires so much effort in preparation. As a result, what should now be quite clear is the fact that there are numerous variables relating to the interview that can be used by researchers to analyze and distinguish between how interviewing is done in various countries.

Finally, the interview is probably the one segment of the news that best represents the interface between the television station on the one hand and the public on the other hand. I mean this in the sense that it is people that the reporters interview, people from many walks of life, including political and social elites as well as simple and ordinary folks. Thus in the interview one can see how the individual non-newsperson is treated by the reporters and the news organizations. This is why the interview is one of the more controversial segments of news broadcasting, since interviewees and audiences alike often claim that the way the interview was presented was unfair and can cause injustice.

This is an interesting point indeed. In my research I have not attempted to document cases in which the way news interviews were conducted have been criticized and even condemned by the interviewees or someone on their behalf. Surely this occurs time and again in all countries. This is partly a result of the unrealistic expectations that the interviewee may have when consenting to be interviewed, and partly due to the way the interviewing process takes place. The interviewee wishes to express his or her opinion but at the same time to guarantee protection from harsh treatment and distortion. The balance required is fragile and perhaps unobtainable. This is why, for example, we often hear of demands to do the interview without any editing.

The interviewee is surely aware of the constraints in the work of the reporter, mainly in terms of the amount of time available for the interview segment. Thus it has been suggested that the interviewee be told how much time he or she has and then be allowed to present his or her case without interruption and without the need to edit what has been said, provided, of course, that the interviewee adhered to the rules of the game. To my knowledge this is not standard practice in television news interviewing, but it could perhaps be considered, mainly in the case of interviews conducted with experts, and possibly with politicians.

One of the earliest analyses of network television news in the United States is the work by Epstein (1973). Epstein suggests (in pages 154-158 of his book) that there are four main reasons why interviews are used in the news: (a) "It makes it possible for the news crew to obtain file footage about an event which they did not attend or which they were not permitted to film"; (b) "it assures that the subject will be filmed under favorable circumstances—an important technical consideration"; (c) "interviews provide an easy means by which an abstract or difficult-to-film concept can be presented in human terms"; and (d) "the interviewing device is probably the easiest way of satisfying the Fairness Doctrine . . . that if one viewpoint is presented on a controversial topic, an opposing one will be presented in the course of a reasonable period of time." I would like to take issue with these points, or at least to suggest that the way interviews are conducted in the news today is only remotely correlated with what Epstein said only 13 years ago. In a general sense I would argue that even if news interviews were conducted in order to satisfy the above four objectives, the way they are presented on the screen, which is surely the critical factor—given that what is shown to the viewers is what really counts—would at best leave us wondering if indeed those were the true motives for the interview.

What I wish to suggest then, is not that Epstein was wrong. Instead, I would suggest two points. First, what Epstein has suggested might be theoretically valid but empirically imprecise. Thus although Epstein could provide a couple of examples of the use of the interview that might substantiate some of his claims, he did not conduct a thorough and systematic content analysis of interviews. While my own analysis did not look at television news interviews done one and two decades ago, but rather focuses on interviews in the mid-1980s, it is my belief that what Epstein claimed back in the early 1970s may not be valid today. This brings me to my second, and more important point, that interviewing, as well as many other facets of television news, has changed over the years, and will most likely keep changing. This change has been brought about by several factors, which clearly have been interacting with one another.

The first factor is the advances made in the technologies of electronic news gathering and the editing possibilities therein. News can be reported from the scene-of-the-event with greater ease than ever before, the news crew can reach more remote locations since the equipment needed has been reduced in size and weight, and editing can be done by the reporter on location without having to return to the studio. This has contributed to the second factor, that is, the increased competition among the news organizations at the national and local levels. Most every local station has its own news department and produces several hours of news daily. One way to create interest in the news is to present information about people and issues with which viewers are familiar. This is easier on the local level than on the national level. And interviewing appears to be an ideal way to bring these people into the newscasts. The third factor, the wide selection of television programs available at any point in time, may have also affected how interviewing is done in the news. Not too many years ago, during certain time slots, almost all one could watch on television would be news programs. Today, with the wide and rapidly growing availability of other sources of television contents, including cable, direct satellite broadcasting, and even home video, news producers are being forced to make the news more dramatic, more fast paced (assuming, as they do, that people cannot pay attention to and grasp the contents of longer stories), and in general, more attractive to the audience. Indeed, interviewing in the news can be dramatic and fast paced, hence a perfect recipe for catching the audience.

THE MORAL OF THE STUDY

The perspective chosen for this study was that of comparative research. It is my assumption that the reader is now convinced of the importance of this approach. Despite the fact that television news in Western society is quite similar in terms of its overall format and contents, it seems that the way interviewing is conducted is quite varied and points to the underlying social and cultural factors that differentiate one country from another. As we have shown, in the case of the United States, where there are three commercial networks, there is relatively much similarity among them. On the other hand, the between-country differences were quite substantial and meaningful on many variables.

Although the average length of the interviews varied from country to country, all the reporters with whom I spoke complained of the lack of time. It was not clear from what they said exactly what they would do if they had a few more seconds. Would they, for example, keep the question in the interview? Would they let the interviewee talk a bit longer? Or possibly both? Surely the added interview time would have to be at the expense of something else, particularly in the nearly totally constrained newscasts in the United States. Interestingly, in the literature which we referred to, little if anything is said about the length of the interview and how to go about keeping it to a minimum. Is it really inevitable that the interview be only a few seconds long?

Most of the reporters saw nothing principally wrong with the interviewer entering the news studio, sitting alongside the reporter or anchor, and being interviewed "live." As a matter of fact, several reporters felt that this is the ideal situation, one in which their true skills as broadcast journalists could be practiced and exhibited. This is not done, however, in most cases, in large measure due to the time constraints and the inability (or at least the fear) of the interviewer of not being able to control the situation sufficiently. My own preference is to have at least one "live" interview in the newscast (not including the perfectly rehearsed situation in which the anchor "interviews" one of his own fellow correspondents). This can satisfy the craving of many reporters to do "live" television, which I believe is a sound rationale in and of itself. Also, such a practice could pressure television journalism to improve its performance, since a mistake made on the air in "live" television cannot be rectified. Incidentally, a large percentage of television viewers in the United States, mainly in the western regions of the country, actually view network news as a tape-delayed program. This is despite the fact that the networks in New York usually produce two versions of the evening news, one immediately following the other. In the second version certain substantive as well as stylistic and technical errors which may have occurred in the course of the first feed are corrected, all as part of the great emphasis on the "packaging" of the news. Thus it would be a challenge for television journalism to run some of its interviewing live, which could force the improvement in the quality of the newscast.

Earlier, when discussing the literature, we noted the relatively great emphasis which was put on the preparation of the questions and how they were worded. We also noted the paradox that despite this preaching little, if any, remnants of the question appear in the actual interview. It is, therefore, quite amusing to note that in the most recent best-selling cookbook on journalistic interviewing (Biagi, 1986) the author states, "Often the audience hears the question a broadcast reporter asks, whereas a newspaper reader rarely knows the questions that produce the story" (p. 104). I would like to suggest that this statement is inaccurate, to say the least. In any event, I would like to suggest that some effort be made on the part of reporters to have the question appear in one form or another in the course of the edited interview, at least more than is customary today. This could be done, if not directly, then by paraphrasing the question, even in an abridged manner, so that there is a clear statement of what the respondent was asked. This, I believe, is important for the credibility of the reporter and the news station. Although there is currently no evidence to prove this, I would like to suggest that if the audience knew what the reporter asked the interviewee, there is a greater likelihood that the viewers would not feel that the sound bites are taken out of context. Indeed, the networks and some stations have strict operating standards relating to, among other things, the need to avoid situations whereby editing would create the impression that an interview took place when, in fact, it did not.

EFFECTS OF THE INTERVIEW
ON THE AUDIENCE

Although this book was primarily concerned with the way interviewing is actually done in the news, I believe that I should not end without making some references to the way the interview might affect the viewers. The television news interview, in the way it is presented, is a carefully assembled package of information, tightly drawn and with little redundancy. Indeed, as we have seen, in all the countries the majority of the interviews are even presented without the questions being heard. At times the interview package may even include statements that an individual has made and which were not exactly a response to a question, but it is edited in such a way so that it appears to be a reply (despite the formal guidelines to avoid this practice). The question of interest here is how this and other factors concerning the interview affect the way the viewer processes the information contained in the interview.

This is part of a more general question which has been examined by several researchers, in the past decade or so, namely, how do audience members perceive, understand, recall, and interpret the news (for instance, Graber, 1984; Robinson and Levy, 1986). The bottom line of some of this research is that there are indeed problems in the comprehension of news, no matter how comprehension is defined. This could, of course, be due to various reasons, some having to do with how people deal with the news and some with how the news is presented. Thus, for example, the amount of interest that people have and their motivation to understand the news, as well as how much knowledge they have on the general area and the specific topic being discussed will surely influence what they make of it. The form of presentation, the language used in the news, the context in which the news items are given, the way the visual information is presented, and how it is blended with the verbal information, all these factors presumably influence to some extent what sense people make out of the news.

I am suggesting that the way the information contained in the interview is presented might have a particularly strong influence on how the full news items are perceived and understood. Thus, for example, the fact that the interview is often so brief might put special pressure on the audience to try to understand what is being said. The fact that the questions put to the interviewees often do not appear and the fact that sometimes only parts of sentences are heard can make things difficult. The often visually intense images presented, such as extreme close-up shots, and distracting background information can result in lack of concentration on what is being said. The extremely brief, and often total lack of identification of the person being interviewed, may be confusing and even annoying. How do viewers react when they see a microphone being pushed toward the interviewee or when it is abruptly pulled away? To my knowledge few, if any, specific empirical findings bearing directly on these points are available.

NEWS INTERVIEWING AND BEYOND

This book began with a general theoretical statement about journalistic interviews. It then narrowed in on television interviewing, and focused primarily on interviewing in television news. And yet, it should be clear that I was unable to cover every aspect of such interviewing. Thus, for example, I have not touched upon legal-ethical questions concerning the news interview, such as the practice of reporters to conduct "ambush" interviews with unsuspecting interviewees. This issue is closely related to two often contradictory rights: on the one hand that of the public's right to know and on the other hand the individual's right to privacy. These kinds of issues involving interviewing have come up from time to time in literature such as the *Columbia Journalism Review*.

What I have particularly tried to do in this book is to make the reader (whether student, researcher, or professional journalist) aware of some of the critical aspects of television news interviewing. I have tried to emphasize some theoretical issues related to interviewing as well as empirical findings which give some view of the state of affairs (and of the "art") today. It is my strong belief that by being exposed to, cognizant of, and concerned with the topic, there will ultimately be an improvement in television news, which has been criticized time and again in recent years.

At several points throughout the manuscript reference was made to other formats of television news interviews, other than national news. What can be said about the other formats of news interviews, and about television interviewing in general? It should be clear that the "profile" of interviews in nationally telecast commercial evening newscasts is different from local news or from the more sophisticated news programs such as those on public broadcasting stations. I believe that the concepts and tools that have been suggested here can be put to good use in studying those other forms of news interviewing, as well as totally different formats of interviewing on television.

I am of the opinion that reporters who conduct interviews should be more aware of these points and take them into consideration when doing their interviews. And yet, most of us who teach and study the performance of journalists are aware of two interrelated facts. First, journalists generally don't seem to be too concerned by what the public may think and feel about the way they do their work. Their most important reference group is their colleagues, not their audience. And second, they don't tend to read the academic and professional literature, at least not once they get out of school. I should add parenthetically that I asked the reporters I spoke to whether or not they generally read such literature and the almost unanimous reply was a straightforward "no." Moreover, most said they would not bother reading this book either, although they did indicate, perhaps simply as a gesture of politeness, that they did find the topic rather interesting, important, and even troubling at times.

Thus although I have intentionally refrained in this volume from making any specific suggestion or recommendation as to how I think the interview should be done (except for some brief comments in this chapter), I think it is quite desirable that students of journalism be knowledgeable about these points. Incidentally, it is interesting to note that the attitude toward formal training in news reporting, including the conducting of interviews, is not the same in all the countries I studied. In the United States, for example, there are numerous schools of journalism, many departments of radio or television broadcasting, and special courses in news production, which attract many students across the country. Many news organizations in the United States consider formal training an important professional asset and often even a prerequisite. On the other hand there are countries, including many in Europe, where formal academic training in broadcast journalism is not available, or in any event is not considered as a prerequisite for a career in journalism. This topic has to do with the sociology of professionalization more than it has to do with our present topic, but I think it gives another pertinent perspective on the role of the journalist in society.

REFERENCES

ANDERSON, D. and P. BENJAMINSON (1976) Investigative Reporting. Bloomington: Indiana Univ. Press.

BIAGI, S. (1986) Interviews That Work: A Practical Guide for Journalists. Belmont, CA: Wadsworth.

BOLCH, J. and K. MILLER (1978) Investigative and In-Depth Reporting. New York: Hastings House.

CONRAD, P. (1982) Television: The Medium and Its Manners. Boston: Routledge & Kegan Paul.

DARY, D. (1971) TV News Handbook. Blue Ridge Summit, PA: Tab.

DAVIS, A. (1976) Television: Here Is the News. London: Severn House.

DENNIS, E. and A. ISMACH (1981) Reporting Processes and Practices: Newswriting for Today's Readers. Belmont, CA: Wadsworth.

DENNIS, E. and W. RIVERS (1974) Other Voices: The New Journalism in America. San Francisco: Canfield.

EPSTEIN, E. J. (1973) News from Nowhere: Television and the News. New York: Random House.

FANG, I. E. (1972) Television News. New York: Hastings House.

FIELD, S. (1975) The Mini-Documentary Serializing TV News. Blue Ridge Summit, PA: Tab.

GANS, H. J. (1979) Deciding What's News: A Study of CBS Evening News, NBC Nightly News, Newsweek and Time. New York: Vintage.

GELLES, R. J. (1974) "The television news interview: a field study." J. of Applied Communication Research (Winter-Spring): 31-44.

Glasgow University Media Group (1976) Bad News. London: Routledge and Kegan Paul.

GRABER, D. (1984) Processing the News: How People Tame the Information Tide. New York: Longman.

GREEN, M. (1969) Television News: Anatomy and Process. Belmont, CA: Wadsworth.

HARTLEY, J. (1982) Understanding News. London: Methuen.

KAHN, R. L. and C. F. CANNELL (1957) The Dynamics of Interviewing. New York: Wiley.

KOCHER, R. (1986) "Bloodhounds or Missionaries: Role Definitions of German and British Journalists." European J. of Communication 1 (March): 43-64.

LEWIS, C. D. (1984) Reporting for Television. New York: Columbia Univ. Press.

METZLER, K. (1977) Creative Interviewing. Englewood Cliffs, NJ: Prentice Hall.

MOLLENHOFF, C. (1981) Investigative Reporting. New York: Macmillan.

NEWCOMB, H. (1982) Television: The Critical View. New York: Oxford Univ. Press.

ROBINSON, J. P. and M. R. LEVY (1986) The Main Source: Learning from Television News. Newbury Park, CA: Sage.

SCHNEIDER, F. (1985) "The substance and structure of network television news: an analysis of content features, format features and formal features." Doctoral Dissertation, Syracuse University.

SHOOK, F. (1982) The Process of Electronic News Gathering. Englewood, CO: Morton.

SILLER, R. C. (1972) Guide to Professional Radio and TV Newscasting. Blue Ridge Summit, PA: Tab.

STEVENS, M. (1980) Broadcast News. New York: Holt, Rinehart & Winston.

TUCHMAN, G. (1974) "Making news by doing work: routinizing the unexpected." Amer. J. of Sociology 79 (July): 110-131.

TUCHMAN, G. (1978) Making News: A Study in the Construction of Reality. New York: Free Press.

TYRELL, R. (1972) The Work of the Television Journalist. London: Focal.

YORKE, I. (1978) Television News. London: Focal.

INDEX

ABOUT THE AUTHOR

Akiba A. Cohen is Senior Lecturer at the Communications Institute of the Hebrew University of Jerusalem. He received a bachelor's degree in psychology and sociology at the Hebrew University in 1966, an M.A. in 1971, and a Ph.D. in 1973, both in communication from Michigan State University. He has been at the Hebrew University since 1973. He has had visiting appointments at Michigan State University in 1977, at the University of Minnesota in 1983 and again in 1986, and at the State University of New York at Buffalo in 1985. He has also lectured at various universities, including Michigan State University, University of Pennsylvania, Arizona State University, Vanderbilt University, University of Munich, University of Maryland, Washington State University, and Kent State University.

His main research interest is television news. He also codirected a five-year international study on the presentation and perception of social conflict in television news, which is being prepared for publication. He is the author of over 25 articles published in various journals including the *Journal of Communication, Communication Research, Human Communication Research,* the *Journal of Broadcasting and Electronic Media, Journalism Quarterly,* and the *International Journal of Communication Research.* He coauthored *Almost Midnight: Reforming the Late Night News* (Sage, 1980) and several book chapters. He holds the following editorial positions: Editorial Consultant, the *Journal of Broadcasting* (since 1983); Editorial Board, *Communications: The European Journal of Communication* (since 1986); and Editorial Board, *Communication Yearbooks 9* and *10.*